Distance Education for Language Teachers

Multilingual Matters

Approaches to Second Language Acquisition
  R. TOWELL and R. HAWKINS
Attitudes and Language
  COLIN BAKER
An Education that Empowers
  JEAN RUDDUCK (ed.)
Educational Research in Europe
  JAMES CALDERHEAD (ed.)
Fluency and Accuracy
  HECTOR HAMMERLY
Foundations of Bilingual Education and Bilingualism
  COLIN BAKER
French for Communication 1979-1990
  ROY DUNNING
The Guided Construction of Knowledge
  NEIL MERCER
Language Education for Intercultural Communication
  D. AGER, G. MUSKENS and S. WRIGHT (eds)
Language, Minority Education and Gender
  DAVID CORSON
Le ou La? The Gender of French Nouns
  MARIE SURRIDGE
Life in Language Immersion Classrooms
  ELIZABETH B. BERNHARDT (ed.)
A Parents' and Teachers' Guide to Bilingualism
  COLIN BAKER
Perceptions of Teaching and Learning
  MARTIN HUGHES (ed.)
Reflections on Language Learning
  L. BARBARA and M. SCOTT (eds)
Second Language Acquisition and Language Pedagogy
  ROD ELLIS
Tasks and Language Learning
  GRAHAM CROOKES and SUSAN M. GASS (eds)
Teaching-and-Learning Language-and-Culture
  MICHAEL BYRAM, CAROL MORGAN and colleagues
Working with Bilingual Children
  M. K. VERMA and S. FIRTH (eds)

Please contact us for the latest book information:
Multilingual Matters Ltd,
Frankfurt Lodge, Clevedon Hall, Victoria Road,
Clevedon, Avon BS21 7SJ, England

Distance Education for Language Teachers

A UK Perspective

Edited by
Ron Howard and Ian McGrath

MULTILINGUAL MATTERS LTD
Clevedon • Philadelphia • Adelaide

Library of Congress Cataloging in Publication Data

Distance Education for Language Teachers: A UK Perspective/
Edited by Ron Howard and Ian McGrath
Collection of papers selected from a symposium of the same title
held at the University of Edinburgh in May 1993
Includes bibliographical references and index.
1. Language teachers–Training of–Distance education–Congresses.
2. Teachers–Training of–Distance education–Congresses.
I. Howard, Ron, 1936– . II. McGrath, Ian, 1945–.
P53.85.D57   1995
418′.007–dc20   95-18703

British Library Cataloguing in Publication Data

A CIP catalogue record for this book is available from the British Library.

ISBN 1-85359-292-7 (hbk)
ISBN 1-85359-291-9 (pbk)

Multilingual Matters Ltd

UK: Frankfurt Lodge, Clevedon Hall, Victoria Road, Clevedon, Avon BS21 7SJ.
USA: 1900 Frost Road, Suite 101, Bristol, PA 19007, USA.
Australia: P.O. Box 6025, 83 Gilles Street, Adelaide, SA 5000, Australia.

Typeset by Formatvisual Ltd, Weston-super-Mare.
Printed and bound in Great Britain by the Cromwell Press.

Contents

Foreword

Distance education for many years was associated with the earnest endeavour of the correspondence course. Aspiring midshipmen amongst *Boys' Own Paper* readers, would-be novelists, those suffering from 'butterfly brains' or 'ashamed of their English' have all enrolled on such courses — David Hume sought help to rid his writing of 'Scotticisms' in the eighteenth century. Now advances in telecommunications have extended the range and interactivity of distance education to make it a more attractive alternative to traditional modes for those with the luxury of choice and a more powerful educative tool for the many with no choice.

The Institute for Applied Language Studies, the University of Edinburgh, (IALS) first became involved in distance education with an ESU prize-winning report-writing course for accountants. This was followed by a distance course for language teachers leading to the RSA Diploma in the Teaching of Foreign Languages to Adults. The next step was to develop a course for teachers of English, and the Advanced Certificate in ELT (by distance learning) was launched in 1992.

The symposium on which this volume is based represents a further development for IALS. It arose from the enthusiasm of two members of IALS staff — Ian McGrath (Teacher Education Co-ordinator) and Ron Howard (Distance-learning Co-ordinator). It provided a rare opportunity for those in the UK with a working interest in the field to present current research and practice. Most of those present were language teacher trainers, in English as a Foreign Language or in modern languages like French, but the articles will be of interest to all who are involved in teacher education at a distance, whatever their subject area. At the same time, these articles are recommended to language teachers who have not yet had experience of distance education since, with the ever increasing demand for education and training, and in the current economic situation, distance education is likely to play a part in more and more language-teaching contexts.

The symposium is the first in a series of IALS symposia for language teacher educators. In 1994 the topic will be issues in the training of teachers of languages for special purposes. As in this case, the proceedings will be published.

Eric H Glendinning, Director, IALS   July 1994

Contributors

Elspeth Broady, University of Brighton
Elspeth is Course Leader of the MA in Media-Assisted Language Learning and Teaching at the University of Brighton. She has recently been involved as a consultant on the French language course being produced by the BBC/OU.

David Carver, Moray House Institute of Education, Edinburgh
David's interests include TEFL in the curricular context, and teacher education for TEFL. He is currently involved in the development of a distance MA TESOL.

John Cowan, Open University in Scotland
John is Director of the Open University in Scotland, former Professor of Engineering Education at Heriot-Watt University, and for 25 years a committed advocate of individualised learning, in as open a form as possible.

Tim Graham, Sheffield Hallam University
Tim is Course Leader for the TESOL Centre's Certificate in TESOL. He has recently developed a new course (with a substantial distance-learning component) for teachers of English to Young Learners.

Beverley Hallam, University of York
At the time of the Symposium Beverley was a Research Fellow at the University of York. She is now a teacher in the Department of Modern Languages at Queen Ethelburga's School, York.

Teresa Haworth, Sheffield Hallam University
Teresa combines a background in Italian teaching with an interest in TESOL. Her particular areas of interest include the development of 'teacher awareness' amongst newcomers to the profession, classroom language and the teaching of writing skills.

Ron Howard, University of Edinburgh
Ron is Development Coordinator for Distance Learning at IALS. His main contributions to teacher education courses are on ESP, especially English for Medicine, and computer assisted language learning. He has directed or participated in workshops for ESP teachers in China, Poland, Hungary, Egypt, and Cuba.

Christina Howell-Richardson, University of Surrey
Christina is a lecturer at the English Language Institute, University of Surrey. She is currently doing research on the use of computer-conferencing in a distance Master's programme.

Charles Jennings, Southampton Institute of Higher Education
Charles is Consultant, Telematic Systems, at CECOMM, Southampton Institute. His work includes the development of courses that introduce educationalists of all disciplines to telematics. He has worked with language teachers in the UK, France, Germany, Hungary and Australia.

Robert Leach, National Extension College
Robert is Assistant Director (Education) of the National Extension College, where he is responsible for the development and running of a wide range of distance-learning courses. He has written a number of print and video resources for EF/SL.

Ian McGrath, University of Edinburgh
Ian is Development Coordinator for Teacher Education at IALS. In recent years his general interest in the methodology of teacher education has found a specific focus in the development of distance-learning courses for practising language teachers.

Gary Motteram, University of Manchester
Gary has taught both in the public and private sector overseas and in Britain. His main interests are now in the uses of educational technology in language learning.

Hélène Mulphin, Open University
Hélène is a lecturer in Modern Languages at the Open University. She has extensive experience in teacher training and teaching French and Spanish, and has written video courses for both languages.

Ray Parker, Sheffield Hallam University
Ray is Course Leader for the TESOL Centre's Postgraduate Diploma in TESOL and for Associated Diploma courses aimed at 'non-native' English language teachers overseas, both of which include substantial distance learning elements.

Dr Hilary Perraton, Commonwealth Secretariat
At the time of writing, Hilary was working in the Commonwealth Secretariat education programme. He has long experience of distance education, having previously worked for both the National Extension College and the International Extension College.

Keith Richards, Aston University
Keith is a lecturer in the Language Studies Unit at Aston University. Between 1987 and 1992 he was responsible for the Unit's international Distance Learning MSc programme in Teaching English.

Gillian Walsh, University of Manchester
Gillian has taught in Colombia and the UK. She is currently working on the distance-learning TESOL programme in the Centre for English Language Studies in Education (CELSE).

Richard West, University of Manchester
After teaching in Zambia and Iran, Richard worked in materials development and teacher training. He is currently Director of CELSE and has been co-ordinator of the distance TESOL programme since 1988.

Introduction

RON HOWARD AND IAN MCGRATH

In 1983, the number of UK institutions offering distance-learning programmes for language teachers could be counted on two or three fingers of one hand; at the time of writing, some 15 such courses are being advertised in the press and elsewhere.

A number of factors have probably led to this dramatic increase.

(1) *An increasing demand for qualifications of at least initial level.* This has encouraged public-sector institutions to develop certificate programmes, validated by an examination board, which combine face-to-face and distance-learning components; it has also encouraged a much larger number of private operators to set up relatively cheap programmes delivered solely through distance learning. For overseas teachers keen to obtain British qualifications, the latter have the obvious appeal of convenience.

(2) *Falling applications for full-time master's courses.* The universities have for some time been experiencing a decline in student numbers on master's programmes resulting from increased competition, the rising costs of full-time courses in the UK, and budget cuts and policy changes in the major funding agencies. Some universities have reacted by developing modular programmes that can be completed over a number of years; others have diversified into distance learning or created totally new master's programmes by distance learning.

(3) *The recognition by public-sector institutions of a need for flexible programmes between certificate and master's level.* This has influenced the development of open-enrolment advanced certificates or diplomas, validated by either an examination board or the institution, and of special programmes based on particular overseas countries.

The various forms of provision can be summarised in the following diagram.

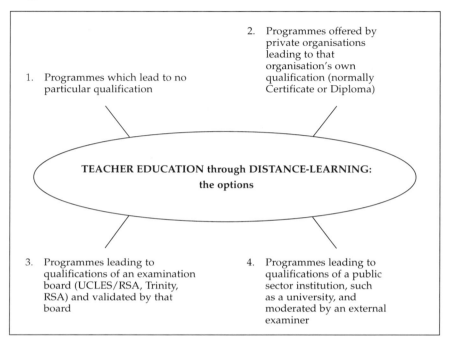

1. Programmes which lead to no particular qualification

2. Programmes offered by private organisations leading to that organisation's own qualification (normally Certificate or Diploma)

TEACHER EDUCATION through DISTANCE-LEARNING: the options

3. Programmes leading to qualifications of an examination board (UCLES/RSA, Trinity, RSA) and validated by that board

4. Programmes leading to qualifications of a public sector institution, such as a university, and moderated by an external examiner

Non-certificated programmes (Category 1) available at the time of writing are few in number, but cover quite a range. They include:

1.1 A 'taster' programme (consisting of booklet plus video) for those who wish to get a feel for language teaching before deciding whether to invest in a more extended programme.

1.2 A revision programme for those preparing for the written papers of an examination for teachers.

1.3 Support/induction programmes for those preparing to teach using a particular approach or specific materials.

1.4 Development programmes for those who feel they would like to improve their understanding of a particular aspect of language teaching.

With the possible exception of 1.2, none of the programmes in category 1 makes claims to be anything other than educationally beneficial, and those in 1.3 may even be free.

By contrast, the certificated programmes in Categories 2–4 offer the prospect of both educational and career development.   One of the distinctions between these three categories centres on who validates the qualification; another is that only Category 3 provides evidence, through the assessment of teaching practice, of classroom competence. The hard fact is that some qualifications are worth more than others, and those that have a higher value in the eyes of informed consumers are inevitably those which — on the basis of the status of the qualification and/or the institution awarding the qualification — are most highly regarded by employers. For those who have no access to information about the relative status of qualifications or institutions, however, there is a real problem of choice.

The Symposium

An awareness of these changes in the pattern of provision had led one of us to express concern at an IATEFL/ALL conference about the validity of the qualifications offered by some of the private operators (McGrath, 1992); it subsequently led us to organise a symposium in Edinburgh under the title 'Distance Education for Language Teachers — a UK Perspective' at which, it was hoped, all the UK institutions offering courses would be represented.

The symposium, the first UK meeting of this kind, took place in May 1993. It had three stated aims:

- to give those working in the field the opportunity to meet and discuss their work and their courses with colleagues from other institutions;
- to provide a forum for the presentation of current ideas and research;
- to provide, through the publication of the symposium papers, an overview for those unable to attend the symposium of the present situation and of future prospects.

The last of these aims perhaps merits some comment. Although there is a considerable literature on distance education in general, much of which is relevant to language-teacher education (for example, Perraton, 1993), the growth in distance-education opportunities for language teachers has not been accompanied by a corresponding growth in published accounts of practitioners' experience or of research in this area. Up to the time of the Edinburgh symposium, the only publication of any substance had been a collection of reports in the British Council *English Studies* series (Number 7, 1991), and this was not widely available. Since then, the first book on the subject of distance learning and ELT (Richards & Roe, 1994) has appeared, as has the report of the British Council Dunford Seminar on language issues in distance education (British Council, 1993); nevertheless, the discipline-specific literature remains sparse. The articles in this collection, which range from theoretical discussion to small-scale case studies, should therefore help to fill this gap by offering an insight into some of the work and thinking in UK institutions today.

Overview

The present volume is a selection from papers presented at the symposium, revised where appropriate in the light of subsequent developments. They are devoted to language-*teacher education*, and deal only peripherally with language *teaching* (although language improvement for teachers is clearly an important concern).

The 15 chapters included are by writers working within major UK institutions concerned with distance education and language-teacher education at a distance: the Open University, and its recently established Centre for Modern Languages, the Commonwealth Secretariat, the National Extension College, the universities of Aston, Brighton (formerly Brighton Polytechnic), Edinburgh, Manchester, Surrey, and York, Sheffield Hallam University (formerly Sheffield City Polytechnic), Moray House Institute of Education (now part of Heriot-Watt University), and Southampton Institute of Higher Education.

The chapters move from the general to the more specific and back to the more general as part of a thematic progression. The 'book-end' chapters by Cowan (Open University) and Carver (Moray House) take a broad view of, respectively, the advantages and disadvantages of distance education and its future, while the second paper, by Perraton (Commonwealth Secretariat), provides a sweeping review of overseas programmes for teachers and their effectiveness. Of the remaining chapters, some address general issues in distance education from the perspective of language-teacher education; others adopt a case-study approach and offer tentative conclusions based on their findings.

Advantages and disadvantages

The collection begins with Cowan's consideration (Chapter 1) of the advantages and disadvantages of distance education in general. A distance-learning course may be the only possibility for learners who, for various reasons, are unable to attend a conventional course. But there are more positive aspects to distance education, and Cowan draws on his experience to review benefits and drawbacks from the perspective of both learner and teacher.

Assuming that distance learning is also normally *open* learning, Cowan reminds us that distance learners have greater freedom than their conventional counterparts to choose what, when, where and how to learn. For example, the distance learner can set thè pace of his or her learning. There is, of course, another side to that coin. As Cowan points out: 'Once learners are freed to study at their own pace, then the prospect of bringing a group together...rapidly becomes less and less feasible.' In general, distance education means reduced contact with peers and with tutors, often resulting in a sense of isolation. Furthermore, the distance learner 'does not have the same opportunity to be aware that the difficulties which she or he is encountering are shared by others, and are not merely an indication of personal incompetence'(p. 17). These disadvantages can be overcome to a large extent by providing adequate support for the learner, as other chapters demonstrate (Broady; Haworth and Parker, for example).

Important as it is to counteract the drawbacks, designing a good distance-education programme is equally a matter of exploiting its potential.

Exploiting the potential

One advantage of distance education that is stressed in a number·of chapters is the possibility for learners 'to draw on resources available in the world outside the classroom' (p. 16). Distance education permits learners to continue working, and apart from the personal benefits arising from this, there is a significant professional advantage for the teacher-learner. Outside the 'classroom' of the course, there is the classroom of the workplace, and for teachers this second classroom, where theories can be tested and new ideas put into practice, will be a particularly important resource (McGrath).

A distance-education course also allows more time for reflection, and this may result in deeper and therefore more effective learning (Cowan; Leach; McGrath; Haworth and Parker). The measured effectiveness of distance education for teachers is one of the topics dealt with by Perraton (Chapter 2). His paper reports mainly on overseas projects; some of these are very large-scale and the results are therefore particularly significant. In Pakistan, 83,000 primary-school teachers were taught about a new curriculum through correspondence lessons and radio programmes; and in Tanzania, 45,000 teachers were enrolled on a distance-learning programme between 1976 and 1981. Studies of these projects indicate that where the number of students reached is the criterion of effectiveness distance learning has a clear advantage over conventional programmes.

But that of course is not the only criterion.

One study cited by Perraton tested samples of trainee teachers of different subjects and found measurable learning gains particularly among *language* teachers studying at a distance. In another study, which looked at examination results, it was found that 'where distance students follow their courses to the end they tend to achieve as good examination results as other part-time students' (p. 29). Both these findings apply to *knowledge* gains; there is as yet no evidence of effectiveness with regard to teaching skills but, as Perraton points out, this limitation is equally true of contact courses.

Administration

Leach (Chapter 3) describes three different models of administration for distance education courses, all three in use by the National Extension College (NEC). These vary in details such as whether NEC operates alone or with a partner institution, whether or not they are involved in assessment and accreditation, and whether students can control their own pacing or have to work in lockstep. At the moment NEC is experimenting with a fourth model, specifically intended for teacher education, which draws on elements of the other three to provide maximum flexibility.

Leach believes that any of these models could be used in language teacher education. 'All the models,' he writes, 'share features which are designed to empower learners' (p. 44). This is a particular strength.

Learner autonomy

Learner autonomy is seen by virtually all contributors to this volume as an attribute that arises naturally, but not effortlessly, out of distance education. Many of the participants on the RSA Diploma course Broady (Chapter 4) describes had difficulty making themselves independent of authority and learning from their own experience. Broady suggests that this was largely due to the loss of 'the regular discussions with tutors and peers that are available on face-to-face courses'. 'It is often,' she continues, 'in talking about teaching with peers (. . .) that students gain confidence in experimenting and reflecting on new ideas' (p. 50). As a result, in the contact phase of the course, she found herself faced with a choice between relieving anxiety, by offering prescriptions, for example, and promoting independence, by helping participants to work out their own solutions. Broady suggests a number of techniques for helping to develop confidence and autonomy in distance learners without increasing anxiety. One of these is to weight assessed work in favour of tasks that encourage a process rather than a product focus — for example, the keeping and analysing of learner diaries.

Haworth and Parker (Chapter 6) also stress the need to foster the autonomy engendered by distance education. They too advocate the writing up of a learner diary, or teaching journal. During the contact phase in their courses at Sheffield Hallam University, they make generous provision of self-managed time. 'Best-lesson workshops', 'teaching-liaison meetings', and 'post-lesson debriefings' are all designed to encourage participants to accept responsibility for their own learning.

Distance vs face-to-face

Contributors to this book also seem to be agreed that, for certain categories of teacher and for certain purposes, distance education may be more appropriate than face-to-face teaching. McGrath (Chapter 5), for instance, asserts that a distance-only continuing education course 'is more likely to be successful in promoting steady long-term change than a programme with comparable content which is delivered face-to-face' (p. 70). When it comes to pre-service training, however, he argues strongly in favour of a 'mixed-mode' programme, since 'four-week face-to-face programmes may not provide a satisfactory theoretical grounding. The distance-only programmes, on the other hand, lack the crucial dimension of classroom practice' (p. 74). Like Broady, he acknowledges that 'one of the most crucial contributions of a face-to-face component may be its power to provide reassurance and support for the individual' (p. 75). For Perraton, experience seems to confirm 'the legitimacy of an approach which combines distance, elements of face-to-face study and supervised teaching practice' (p. 30). Haworth and Parker put the case for mixed mode more colourfully: 'If forced, we can all choose between strawberries and cream but we would hardly see one as an alternative to the other and most people would see the benefit of combining the flavours' (p. 90).

There is less consensus on the relative proportions of distance and contact teaching and on their sequencing. To some extent this is again dependent on the type of course, whether it is initial teacher training or a postgraduate degree course, for example. But even with similar courses, different combinations and sequences have been tried and found effective. The RSA/Cambridge Dip. TEFLA run by International House, London begins with a face-to-face induction course, whereas the Trinity College courses offered by Sheffield Hallam University begin with a distance module. Comparative studies would be useful, although it may well turn out that both sequences have their advantages.

The role of technology

Materials for distance-learning courses have in the past been predominantly print-based, and, the Open University apart, delivery in Britain has been mainly via the postal service. This has been the case with teacher education as with other types of course, but circumstances are changing. Audio and video materials are increasingly part of the package, and now computing is also being used although still, at this stage, mainly in courses on educational technology. Motteram (Chapter 7) describes a module on Computer Assisted Language Learning (CALL) which is part of an M.Ed. degree course at Manchester. Some of the material for this module is on disk in a hypertext form, and it is planned to extend the use of computer-based learning to other modules in the near future. Eventually, the whole course will be available in multimedia format on CD-ROM.

Radio and television have long been used by the Open University. The OU, in Scotland especially, has made extensive use of the telephone as a way of providing tutorial support, and the use of the telephone for counselling has become more widespread (Mulphin). More recent developments include the use of satellite television, fax as an alternative to the postal service for delivering print-based materials and for student–tutor contact, and computers linked through the telephone network.

Computer conferencing, which allows distance learners to interact through such networks, is now being used at the Institute of Education in London. As described by Howell-Richardson (Chapter 9), the characteristics of the interaction are intriguing. For example, because 'many of the paralinguistic and social cues relied upon to make inferences about the context, fellow participants and management of the interaction are filtered out', Howell-Richardson explains, '. . . certain politeness constraints are weakened' with the result that 'uninhibited personal behaviour is not unknown ... and can take the form of over-harsh reactions to others' comments' (p. 121). Another feature is the increased opportunity to participate; this sometimes means that computer conferencing groups have difficulty reaching decisions. The nature of this interaction and the factors that affect it are not yet fully understood but Howell-Richardson offers tentative recommendations for tutors using the technology, advice that more and more language teacher educators will need before long.

Many of the newest forms of technology, including computer conferencing, satellite television and video conferencing, are already being used to teach students on a Berlitz English for Bankers course. Tutors are trained to use these media, appropriately enough, through the media themselves. Jennings (Chapter 8) describes the 'virtual classroom' which results, and claims that the main obstacles to using these technologies are organisational and pedagogic. He foresees the 'development of full multimedia communication networks which can offer a platform for rich communication forms including text, sound, voice, image, video and other multimedia elements' (p. 113), but exciting as these technological advances are, he advises a 'cautious and balanced approach' (p. 115) to their introduction.

Caution is certainly necessary when considering the use of technology in developing countries, where the need for distance learning is especially acute. In relation to teacher-training programmes for language teachers in overseas contexts, language improvement is a particular concern. Apart from the high-tech proposals put forward by Jennings, no techniques for language improvement at a distance are discussed in this volume, but this is clearly an issue that course providers overseas have had to address. Some exchange of working solutions, as proposed in the Postscript to this introduction, seems desirable.

Print-based materials

Even print-based materials have been influenced by new technology. Word processing and desktop publishing have brought about an improvement in readability, and have made revision and updating of materials easier. However, there is still much that can be done to improve materials.

West and Walsh (Chapter 10), for instance, stress the importance of producing teaching materials that encourage interaction between the learner and the writer/tutor. Learners must first 'deconstruct' input text, assimilate it into existing schemata, and then, at the appropriate time, 're-construct' it to produce their own output. They suggest that these processes can be facilitated by giving learners a text that is already partially 'deconstructed', for example a text with some of the key words removed, and by providing partially 're-constructed' text in the tasks. Tasks, e.g. Self Assessment Questions (SAQs), are essential both in facilitating the processing of texts and in providing learners with feedback on the effectiveness of their processing. West and Walsh categorise SAQs into a variety of different types, each having specific functions. They then go on to suggest that the proportion of different task types should vary systematically as learners progress through each unit.

A number of authors have provided guidelines for making the language of distance-learning materials more accessible to readers, but as Richards (Chapter 11) points out, these guidelines pay little or no attention to discourse structure. Richards shows how linguistic analysis can lead both to a diagnosis of the problem and to improvements in materials. In his study, two modules in an MA course were analysed. On the face of it there seemed little to distinguish the two and yet one consistently received negative feedback from students. When prompted, students complained specifically of a variety of features including 'excessive use of quotation marks, bold face type, parentheses and italics for emphasis, reference, examples' (p. 147). Detailed analysis, however, failed to show any significant difference between the two modules in any of the features mentioned by students. In fact, the problem lay in the discourse structure of the unpopular module.

Evaluation

One implication of Richards' study is that student criticism cannot always be taken at face value. That is not, of course, to underrate the importance of student feedback in the on-going evaluation of materials and methods. Richards used several techniques for obtaining information from students including standard evaluation forms in each component file. Broady obtained 'indirect' feedback from the personal portfolios of her students. Parker and Graham (Chapter 12) collected information in four different ways at Sheffield Hallam University: during the distance-learning phase using two different techniques, and with questionnaires, once at the end of the distance phase, and once at the end of the contact phase. They conclude that neither the timing nor the particular technique seem to be crucial, but on a 'belt and braces' principle it may be advisable to use more than one. Examples of responses from students on their Certificate in TESOL courses are included in the chapter.

Student feedback in the earliest stages of course development is also obviously useful though not always easy to obtain. Many course developers have to rely simply on feedback from colleagues, but a large organisation like the Open University pilots its materials and also receives advice from external experts (Mulphin).

Modern-language teaching

Although the majority of the chapters in this collection deal with distance education for teachers of English, they are of equal relevance to teachers of other languages and, indeed, three chapters concern the modern-language teacher directly. Broady writes about a course leading to the RSA Diploma for Teachers of Foreign Languages to Adults, while Mulphin (Chapter 13) provides interesting insights into the process of developing materials for the eagerly awaited Open University French language course (due to be launched in February 1995) and describes the components of the supporting Tutor Pack.

Hallam (Chapter 14) reports on materials produced at the University of York and Homerton College, Cambridge, for teachers of French. These comprise *Learning Strategies*, a professional development course (video cassette, audio cassettes, and teacher's manual), and accompanying materials for classroom exploitation. The course is 'intended in the first instance for qualified language teachers who left the classroom some years ago' (p. 183) and who are returning to teach secondary school French. Hallam and her colleagues, conscious of the need for additional support for teachers using the materials, made use of a network of local centres and set up the possibility for users to communicate with each other electronically as well as by more conventional means.

Quality control

In the final chapter, Carver returns to a more general and theoretical level of discussion in his consideration of quality in language teaching and teacher education. He argues that the 'industrialisation' of distance education need not be at odds with the prevailing humanistic approach to language teaching, and that what is required is a reconciliation between 'economy, efficiency and effectiveness' on the one hand and the concepts that can be subsumed under the heading 'learner-centredness' on the other. He concludes with the inspiring suggestion that, 'as distance education has impacted in a major way on traditional higher education, so perhaps, in a less dramatic way, language teaching might contribute to the emerging reconceptualisation of distance education' (p. 204).

Recurring Themes and Research Questions

Despite the differences in approach and focus, it is possible to discern in the various chapters a number of recurring issues or themes, which may be the best indicator of what we have called 'the UK perspective'. These include:

- the relationship between distance and face-to-face education, and the respective contribution of distance and face-to-face components to programmes for language teachers;
- inherent features of distance education (e.g. isolation, delay, reflection, autonomy) and ways in which these can be counteracted or positively exploited;
- the nature of interactivity between participants and materials and

the potential contribution — and limitations — of high technology delivery systems;

• the contribution of an experiential, distance-learning element to *tutor* training;

• quality control and measures of effectiveness.

Certain of these themes will no doubt form part of the research and development agenda over the next few years.

Other items for that agenda would include the following:

Motivation and drop-out

Programme organisers and participants report that motivation starts high and then dips. Why? Does it matter if most people come out of the decline with new resolve? Can anything be done to prevent the dip altogether? Institutions offer various forms of contact with tutors, but these are not necessarily used by students. Why not? In some cases, the decline in motivation continues and results in drop-out. What is the difference between those who continue and those who drop out. Is the issue one of support on the part of the peer group or the institution? Can potential drop-outs be identified in advance? Should the entrance requirements for distance-education programmes be the same as for face-to-face programmes? more rigorous? Diaries may be one method of gaining some insight into changes in participants' attitudes over time and what causes these.

Study skills training

Many programmes incorporate a study-skills element for those who have been away from formal education for some time or who have never had such training. Typical components would include advice on note-taking and academic writing but also guidance on how to organise one's time. Should study-skills components form part of the induction material for all programmes? Are there particular discipline-specific study skills that should be emphasised in programmes for language teachers or is the main distinction related to the level of the programme and the form of assessment? Informal reports suggest that even where a study-skills component is included there may still be a tendency on the part of both native and non-native speakers of English to rely heavily and uncritically on what are taken to be authoritative sources. The extent to which distance education encourages autonomy on the one hand and causes dependency on the other is a question raised by Broady (Chapter 4) that merits further investigation.

Effectiveness

There is some evidence that distance education can produce certain effects on teachers, as Perraton notes (Chapter 2) : what is less clear is the nature of the interaction between the distance component (as opposed to such practical elements as observation or micro/practice teaching) and participants' teaching in their own classrooms. What kinds of input are most likely to be applied and what stimulates their application? Do ideas or advice that conflict with the participants' own views tend to be rejected or do they cause destabilisation? Again, diaries or teaching logs might be an appropriate method of investigation.

Postscript

When we circulated the call for papers for the symposium, we had expected to receive proposals relating to, for instance, the use made of audio and videotapes (an obvious way of providing samples of teaching for analysis), and the relationship between specially written material and set readings (extracts or full-length works), a convenience in any programme for teachers and a necessity in master's programmes. We had also anticipated interest in organisational features of programme and materials design; assessment and credit accumulation; the structure of a unit of material; graphic design. All institutions must consider these questions — and others, such as feedback mechanisms, library resources, costing. It is our hope that the publication of this book will stimulate further exchange at this practical level as well as the research and model-building that will be necessary if UK institutions are to make a contribution to language teacher education on the world scene.

References

British Council (1991) *Distance Learning.* English Studies, Issue No. 7. London: The British Council.
British Council (1993) *Language Issues in Distance Education.* Dunford Seminar Report 1993. London: The British Council.
McGrath, I. (1992) Teacher education through distance learning: a matter of faith? Paper presented at IATEFL/ALL Conference, Edinburgh, April 1992 .
Perraton, H. (ed.) (1993) *Distance Education for Teacher Training.* London: Routledge.
Richards, K. and Roe, P. (eds) (1994) *Distance Learning in ELT.* London: Modern English Publications/The British Council.

1 The Advantages and Disadvantages of Distance Education

JOHN COWAN

My views on distance education emerge from my own first-hand experience both as a learner and as a tutor, in technology, science, social sciences and in theology. I offer them for questioning *and testing out*, by those who are concerned with distance learning in language-teacher education. I hope such readers may find it helpful to reflect on the nature of their teaching, to identify where it is — and is not — similar to other distance learning, and to consider what experience may be transferable.

Distance Learning

I'm rather liberal in the way I interpret the term 'distance learning'. I take it to encompass those situations in which teacher and learners are located in different places, for much if not all of the time. By that definition, the Open University offers distance learning; so, too, does the University of Aberdeen — when a lecturer in Aberdeen teaches a class group in the Orkney Islands, using an electronic whiteboard; and so, too, does a Learning Resource Centre wherein materials are used by learners whose 'teachers', having prepared their resource materials, are now working in their staff rooms on another floor of the same building.

Usually separation by distance gives learners freedom to work at their own pace and in their own separate ways; but this is not always true — as evidenced by the University of Aberdeen example in the previous paragraph. For the moment, however, I will restrict myself to the large majority of situations in which distance can be equated with at least some dimensions of open-ness in learning. I take 'open learning' to imply situations in which learners have the opportunity to exercise choice between valid and significant options that affect their learning, in respect of pace, content, method or standards; or where access to learning, through the specification of prerequisite coverage or qualification, is unrestricted or relatively 'open'. Thus, as I will argue later, most distance learning situations — by virtue of the fact that they leave the teacher without direct control — are essentially 'open' in the first sense of my use of that descriptor. It does not necessarily follow that all distance learning is open in that way, for it is possible for learning at a distance to be tightly structured and controlled by the teacher — but that is unusual.

In relation to the second of my types of open-ness, namely the absence of prerequisite requirements, this is possible in both distance learning and face-to-face courses.

Advantages

What, then, are the advantages of distance and open learning?

Let me begin on a personal note. As a learner, I have experienced many advantages in open learning at a distance. First of all, I can study at my own pace, I can spend time over something that puzzles or intrigues me, before I proceed. That's something I cannot do if the teacher controls the pace of my learning, and particularly if the teacher controls the pace of a class group — who may not all be experiencing the same difficulties, or interests, as I am. In distance learning I can arrange my week to suit my work and family commitments; I can schedule my studies at times that would be awkward or unsuitable for you as my teacher, and for my fellow students. I can allow other commitments to delay my studies by a week or more, provided I make time thereafter to catch up on my studies, before I encounter one of your fixed deadlines. I control pace to a great extent.

Once learners have discovered, as I did, the options that their control over the pace of their learning makes possible for them, they should begin to realise that they can now control the way in which they learn. If they're the kind of person who likes to commence study from the end, rather than from the beginning, then they may do so. There *are* learners like that around; for them such 'retrogressive chaining' *does* prove effective. If, on the other hand, they like to spend time acquainting themselves with the context of study before filling in the fine details, then they may follow that entirely respectable style of learning. If they find it more effective to make two swift passes through the materials, rather than one long and thorough progression (or vice versa), then again these options are open to them. I would hope that teachers will encourage learners to check the effectiveness of whatever choices they make about modes of study. But teachers should remember that learners who have long had to conform to whatever style of learning was assumed in their previous teachers' presentation of courses can benefit enormously from autonomy about the route they follow to learning — provided they exercise that autonomy thoughtfully and evaluate their decisions objectively.

The open-ness that comes with distance offers learners yet more options. As they explore the freedom that distance makes possible, they begin to realise that they can control the content and emphasis of what they study, to a lesser if not a greater extent. If there's a part of the course that bores them, or which they cannot master, or for which they can see no purpose (for them, at least), or in which they are already competent, then they can skip past it without a second thought — and transfer the time saved to parts of the course that they deem more worthy of their attention. They could not do that in a course where the pace and progression are controlled by the teacher.

Finally, in a situation where so many decisions are open to the learners and where it is they who will eventually pay the penalty if decisions are not made wisely, it becomes more and more important for them to be clear about what they want to learn (their goals) and to what standard (their criteria). For it is *their* goals and criteria that should influence their choices between options, and their evaluation of the effectiveness of these choices. My experience suggests that those who take on this burden of self-evaluation in a distance-learning context become deeper, as well as more purposeful, learners in consequence.

So far I have listed advantages that I have described essentially from the learner's standpoint. There are also advantages in open and distance learning that are perhaps less directly apparent to the learners, but that a teacher would highlight.

As a teacher in this type of context, I have found it an attraction to be able to air important questions in situations where learners do not immediately demand that their teacher (the authority) should provide the definitive answer or, failing that, will simply look to their classmates for assistance. In distance learning, it can be easier to cajole individual learners to think deeply — by leaving them to do so.

In distance learning, it can also be much easier to arrange for learners to draw on resources available in the world outside the classroom. A decade ago, I often explored the geology of Arthur's Seat and the Salisbury Crags in Edinburgh, with patrols of Boy Scouts. I didn't make the trips myself. I went with them on an audio-tape, played from a Sony Walkman by

Scouts who were using their map-reading skills as well as studying geology. As a student, I have been able to carry my studies of professional judgement into current situations in my employment, where I and my colleagues were exercising professional judgement; I then used that case material in the project work associated with my distance-learning studies. The Open University, of course, provides countless examples of autonomous distance learners who pursue their studies while visiting art galleries, architectural masterpieces, botanical gardens or theatrical performances.

Disadvantages

So far, I've painted a rosy picture, in terms of features that most would see as enhancing learning. I'd better balance the account, now, and write something about the disadvantages of distance and open learning, as I've encountered them.

(1) First and foremost, communication. This inevitably suffers when teacher and learners are in different places. We have a reasonable repertoire of equipment that assists us to minimise this disadvantage nowadays. Through video-conferencing, it is possible for groups to see each other and to speak to each other, on two or more sites. Through teleconferencing, many isolated students have been able to join in group work and in exchanges with a tutor that prove invaluable to them. The fax machine is generally available to, although not always owned by, students. It can be imaginatively used to render routine telephone communication much more effective. Nevertheless, few learners would describe contact at a distance, compared with face-to-face contact, as less than second-best in terms of communication.

(2) Once learners are freed to study at their own pace, then the prospect of bringing a group together (even through the use of technology) rapidly becomes less and less feasible. If it can be arranged for all students at the same point of time, they may not all be at the same stage in their studies. And so the potential of group work in the curriculum suffers accordingly, through the breaking of ranks that scatters the group of learners.

(3) Learning at a distance can be a very isolated experience. One consequence of that isolation is the absence of social links, whose importance in learning is surely under-estimated in conventional situations. The distant learner does not have the same opportunity to be aware that the difficulties which she or he is encountering are shared by others, and are not merely an indication of personal

incompetence. Those brief, helpful and informal contacts between one learner and another, which can do so much to unpick a 'log jam' in learning, are still possible. But they happen less frequently, because phone calls need to be made, and perhaps arranged at suitable times — which are by then unsuitable, as far as the original and usually immediate learning need is concerned.

(4)   Because everything happens at a distance, it follows that sharing, borrowing, returning, issuing and other such functions involving books, paperwork and assignments, take time. The interruptions to learning which that delay introduces can be frustrating and demotivating.

(5)   When learners are at a distance, we notice that as teachers we cannot do things that we took for granted in the face-to-face situation. For example, it is impossible at a distance for the teacher to keep a casual eye on the learner's performance and progress. Distance is furthermore a severe constraint on the development of a relationship, perceived or otherwise, between the teacher and the learner. And distance is a disincentive to corporate activity, and the learning together which often happens naturally and informally in a class.

Distant — But Not Open — Learning

Now, let's return to a distinction I set on one side in my opening comments. What about learning which is distant — but not open?

For the life of me, I cannot see that any of the advantages that I listed earlier would be present without the open-ness that most distance-learning schemes offer. If the learning is teacher-directed, and yet at a distance, I can only see disadvantage — with one exception. For, if the learner would not otherwise be able to study the course or the subject in question, then clearly there is *some* advantage in an arrangement that makes that possible. But I cannot otherwise see attractions in learning at a distance, without doing so in an open-learning mode.

An Assortment of Additional Points

There are other factors I suppose I should mention, to make this summary more complete. There are some features of distance learning that may be advantages or disadvantages — depending on what is being learnt, and at what level.

In the numerate subject areas, for example, and where learners are developing the ability to apply understanding of a method or a principle, anything that *delays* their access to necessary assistance when their progress is blocked is obviously undesirable. On the other hand, where the subject and the level of study demand critical thinking, it may be a considerable advantage for teachers to have a moment to consider and refine their responses, before passing them on to learners; and it may be an even greater advantage for learners if they can digest the response before deciding if and what they wish to question further. That is where computer-mediated communication may well be an attractive alternative to face-to-face tuition.

This is an appropriate point at which to mention pedagogy. I must admit to a strong conviction that, in adult education, we have been regrettably slow to realise that we have many different types of learning goals, and that methods of teaching and learning that are appropriate for one type may be quite inappropriate for another. For example, the purposeful development of the ability to make evaluative judgements is something that will happen when learners are encouraged to reflect constructively on past experiential learning, and theorise and experiment forward into imminent experiences of a similar and more demanding nature. It is not effective to present them with an algorithm or recipe, to explain to them the procedure to be followed, and to expect them to proceed effectively in consequence. Yet that *is* a moderately effective way of helping learners to develop their ability to apply basic understanding, in familiar and oft-repeated procedures that are frequently demanded in many disciplines. Different levels of learning call for different methods of teaching.

Further, in any given subject-area, whether it is languages or otherwise, we are likely to find that a move from face-to-face teaching to distance and open learning will bring with it the opportunity to think afresh about matching the style of the teaching and learning situation to the levels (and domains) of the learning goals. And so we should take time to consider carefully:

- What *are* the relevant needs of our learners, in this subject-area?
- Which of these can be met in the new style of presentation, and how?
- What does that leave unfulfilled on the list of learning needs?
- Are there feasible and reasonably effective ways of trying to provide a minimally adequate response, in the new format? If so, how?

and, finally:

- Will the proposed outcome, overall, match or surpass the status quo?

Note that, when teachers answer the last question, there will clearly be a strong element of speculation and prediction in their judgements. There is also an obligation on them to compare distance learning realistically with a status quo that almost certainly contains its own weaknesses — weaknesses that have been accepted for so long that they tend to be overlooked, although they need not necessarily be present in the proposed style of presentation.

Summary

In *distance learning,* teachers and learners are in different locations.

In *open learning* learners may:

- learn at their own *pace;*
- control the *way* in which they learn;
- control the *content and emphasis* of what they learn;
- control or shape goals and criteria, and *evaluate* the learning.

A teacher in a distance learning situation:

- finds it easier to call for *deep thinking;*
- uses *resources* that are unavailable in the classroom.

Distance learning:

- makes *communication* between teacher and learner more difficult;
- makes *group work* more awkward to arrange at suitable times;
- introduces undesirable *delays* in the learning sequence;
- makes *casual oversight* of learning progress impossible;
- constrains the *teacher/learner relationship;*
- inhibits *corporate activity.*

These are consequences of *open-ness,* rather than of distance.

It is worth exploring the potential of delays in contact for a distance learner.

If:

- the needs of learners;
- the potential of distance format;
- the needs that may not be met;
- possible ways of coping with any gaps between needs and provision

are considered and balanced against each other, distance learning can surely match or surpass the status quo — because of its open-ness.

2 Distance Education for Teacher Training: International Experience

HILARY PERRATON

As neither a linguist nor a teacher educator, I begin by asserting the importance of language and the importance of teachers. For Wittgenstein in 1922 (p. 148), 'the limits of my language mean the limits of my world'. A quarter century later George Orwell interpreted those limits in his appendix on 'The principles of Newspeak' in *Nineteen Eighty-four:*

> The purpose of Newspeak was not only to provide a medium of expression for the world-view and mental habits proper to the devotees of Ingsoc, but to make all other modes of thought impossible ...This was done partly by the invention of new words, but chiefly by eliminating undesirable words and by stripping such words as remained of unorthodox meanings... To give a single example. The word *free* still existed in Newspeak, but it could only be used in such statements as 'This dog is free from lice' or 'This field is free from weeds'. It could not be used in its old sense of 'politically free' or 'intellectually free', since political and intellectual freedom no longer existed even as concepts, and were therefore of necessity nameless (1949: 241–2).

Along with the the intellectual giants of the century I would like to quote a modest researcher, Joseph Trenaman, whose work is closer to a narrow definition of the theme of this collection of papers. He did a classic study comparing the educational effectiveness of print, radio and television. He established that differences between subjects and audiences were more important than differences between media, and concluded with an affirmation of the importance of language, reminding us in relation to television, the most visual medium, that:

even when it is using its visual capacities to the full, television must still rely on language to communicate very much of the meaning of what is seen. And the moment the subject moves away from what is immediately perceived we are entering the field of ideas conveyed through language (1967:112).

Teachers are important as well as language. I have said previously:

Good education demands good teachers. Over the course of the twentieth century, as the teaching profession has grown, so have its standards risen. Many teacher-training courses in rich countries now last for four years and follow after twelve years of schooling: teachers have now had four more years of full-time education than used to be the norm. Society has steadily expected more of teachers in the variety of tasks they have to perform, in the skills they need to master and in the imagination required for their work. Rising expectations have brought rising quality (Perraton, 1993: 1).

Evidence for the rising expectations and steadily improving performance of the teaching profession in England is unequivocal. At a time when the profession has been undervalued, even denigrated, the admirable statistics bulletin of the Department for Education (1992) shows how more children have steadily been getting more passes in GCSE[1] and 'A' levels[2]. Of course, examinations are not the whole story but last year's data show, for example, that in ten years the proportion of school leavers with five or more GCSE passes in the top three grades rose from 24 to 35% for boys and from 26 to 41% for girls. In the same ten years the number of 18-year-olds with two or more 'A' levels went up from 14% of the age group to 22%. Occam's razor would suggest that this is because of the rising standards, and improved qualifications, of the teaching profession.

So distance education for teachers is an important theme. To address it, I want to start with one question to which I think we have the answer: Is distance education any good for teacher training? I shall go on from there to ask what interesting questions come next. In doing so I have two cautions. First, I am talking about teacher education in general rather than about the education of language teachers. Second, most, though not all, of the evidence I am quoting comes from developing rather than industrialised countries. There may be rich-country literature, with which I am less familiar, which contradicts some of it. But I am without apology inferring from poor countries to rich.

The Purposes of Teacher Education

While programmes of teacher education vary in their emphasis, many of them share four aims: to provide a general education; to improve subject knowledge; to teach educational theory; and to show how to teach. At the same time, programmes often reflect a hope — not always realised — that the attitudes of trainees will remain or become positive towards education and towards the philosophy of education that lies behind the programme. For many purposes we can put the first two aims together, distinguishing between subject and general education on the one hand and professional, pedagogical education embracing both theory and practice on the other.

In his classic analysis of the problems facing teacher education in many developing countries Beeby pointed out the connection between the separate elements:

> the distinction between general education and training is not as obvious as might appear.... There is a continuous spectrum stretching from what everyone would agree upon as general education to instruction that is quite clearly professional training. Exactly where the line will be drawn between them depends not only upon the individual making the judgment but also upon the stage of development of the school system and upon the grades at which the trainees in question are going to teach. Knowledge that is quite essential stock-in-trade for the teacher at one level may be thought of rather as part of a teacher's cultural and intellectual background at a different level or in a different setting (1966: 83).

Beeby also stressed the importance of an adequate command of subject matter, and warned that teachers could not expect to teach effectively or well if they were faced with a syllabus beyond the limits of their own understanding.

Although it is less often made, there is also a strong argument for theory. Lionel Elvin put it like this:

> 'theory' is necessary to give the new teacher a framework of ideas without which he will flounder in practice. They are not ideal truths but reasonably well founded working hypotheses. It is of no use saying, for instance, 'Forget all theory, just train teachers to teach children to read' (or whatever it may be). There is no one cause for failure to learn to read. A teacher has to be prepared to deal with a whole series of problems that may arise when Johnny can't read. The explanation may be physical, poor eyesight or defective hearing. The

materials may be unsuitable to his age and interests. There may be emotional disturbance. As soon as you begin to analyse these situations you are in the realm of working 'theory'. If you say 'Throw theory out of the window' you are asking for a teacher who does not think about what he is doing, and you are going to fail him in his work (1974: 145).

The case for the third element of teacher education — to acquire the skills needed to teach effectively in the classroom — is self-evident. At the same time there are programmes of teacher education that for sound reasons do not include any teaching practice. The Open University in Britain, for example, has run programmes of continuing education for trained and qualified teachers that have concentrated on particular educational topics — reading or educational evaluation for example — and have not included a teaching-practice element. It took the view that, as the teachers following its courses were already trained and experienced, it could provide a useful service for them without organising and supervising their classroom practice. A course at a much more basic level for primary school teachers in Kenya concentrated solely on raising their subject mastery as that was seen as the key priority (Hawkridge *et al.*, 1982). But, for the most part, teacher education needs to take account of the need to practise in the classroom some of the skills that are being taught in the course. This has significant practical and logistic implications. Teaching practice needs to be arranged, supervised and examined, at schools that are often physically and organisationally removed from the teachers' college where training is undertaken.

The Challenges

Over and above the difficulties of balancing the three elements that it is likely to contain, teacher education has faced a further series of difficulties. These have been particularly marked in the developing world. The most startling are the numerical imperatives. The speed at which education has grown in the last forty years means that the education profession has itself had to expand at a historically unprecedented rate. The demand for teachers to staff the schools means that the education profession in developing countries has had to recruit a higher proportion of the output from secondary or tertiary education than is the case in the industrialised countries. These numerical imperatives have, in turn, led to a search for ways of rapidly expanding the teaching force. Teacher education faces challenges of costs and of effectiveness along with these challenges of numbers. The World Bank has noticed that, despite the varied aims of teacher education, many programmes have had to make up for the limited basic education of their students by concentrating on what is essentially a secondary-school curriculum. But, typically, the costs of teacher education are far higher than the costs of secondary education so that teachers' colleges are a relatively costly way of providing the equivalent of secondary schooling (Lockheed & Verspoor, 1991: 95).

The effectiveness challenge is as serious. More than ten years ago Schiefelbein and Simmons examined the effect that teacher training had on the subsequent performance of the teachers' students in the classroom:

> In 13 studies the presence of certified teachers in the classroom significantly affected student scores, and in 19 they did not. . . . In the meantime, it is possible to suggest that present methods and duration of teacher training and upgrading should be reviewed with caution as a way to increase student achievement (1981: 25).

More recent reviews suggest the position has not changed. A World Bank review found that 'in many countries, teacher training provides few teaching skills' (Lockheed & Verspoor, 1991: 99). Avalos (1991: 30) concluded that 'there is little evidence about which approaches work best in training teachers to undertake the variety of roles required of them'.

The numerical imperatives, doubts about costs, concern about effects, and a growing commitment to continuing education have together led to an interest in alternative methods of teacher education. One of these is distance education, which has been used both for the initial training of teachers — especially in developing countries — and for their continuing education, in both industrialised and developing countries.

I define distance education as 'an educational process in which a significant proportion of the teaching is conducted by someone removed in space and/or time from the learner' (Perraton, 1982: 4). The phrase 'significant proportion' is important; the definition deliberately assumes that the use of media, like print and broadcasting, may be combined with opportunities for face-to-face study or, in the case of teacher education, with supervised classroom practice. This paper assumes, throughout, that the distant elements are part, but rarely the whole, of distance education.

Because of its technology, distance education enables teachers to be trained without their being taken off the job. Because of the scale at which it can operate, large numbers of teachers can be trained at much the same time. Some distance-education programmes have demonstrated an alternative model of teacher training in which full-time employment as a classroom teacher is combined with professional training. In Zimbabwe, for example, teachers were trained in this way in order to expand the teaching force at great speed after independence.

A recent review of world experience, based both on existing literature and on a series of case studies that examine evidence on costs, methods and effects (Perraton, 1993), suggests some of the answers to questions about how well distance education has performed in comparison with the alternatives.

Effects, Costs and Methods

Educational effectiveness can be measured in various ways. There is some evidence of the outcomes of distance education for teacher training on four kinds of measure: on the audience reached, on learning, on personal benefit, and on classroom performance. And there is evidence on the comparative cost of achieving a particular educational effect.

The first measure — of reach — is the simplest, and of restricted value, but nevertheless of some significance both for planners and for researchers. When Pakistan wanted to teach a large proportion of its 155,000 primary school teachers about a new curriculum, it called on the Allama Iqbal Open University to run a Primary Teachers' Orientation Course that used correspondence lessons and radio programmes. Over ten course cycles it enrolled 83,000 teachers (Robinson, 1993: 234), a larger number than would have been possible through any other method. Similarly the Department of Education and Science called on the British Open University to develop a training pack about new national examinations that was distributed to all secondary schools in England and Wales (Prescott & Robinson, 1993: 293). Many programmes of teacher education have been smaller than this: African programmes run in the 1960s and 1970s typically had between 600 and 3,000 students and the Tanzanian programme with 45,000 enrolled between 1976 and 1981 was very much the exception (cf. Perraton, 1986). The evidence is limited but clear: distance education can reach students in significant numbers both in industrialised countries with sophisticated communication systems and in developing countries with simpler systems and fewer resources.

The evidence that students learned effectively is more limited and is of two kinds. A small number of studies have tested samples of students in order to measure the learning gained at a distance. Comparative research in Sri Lanka and Indonesia found evidence of learning gains for trainee teachers studying at a distance but suggested that learning in mathematics and the sciences posed greater problems than in other subjects and, of particular interest to us, greater problems than in teaching languages, where the results were comparatively good (Nielsen & Tatto, 1993: 126–7). Where trainee teachers have taken similar examinations to those taken by students following regular, face-to-face courses it is possible to compare the two groups. There is comparable evidence of examination success from open and bimodal universities offering degree programmes. The evidence is consistent: where distance students follow their courses to the end they tend to achieve as good examination results as other part-time students. Many teacher-training programmes have guaranteed their students enhanced status and improved pay on completion and, in consequence, have also achieved high completion rates. Given a supportive environment, students working at a distance can reach examination success levels that are comparable with alternatives (cf. Perraton, 1993: 393).

We can also legitimately ask whether trainee teachers get what they want out of programmes of distance education. Again, evidence is limited but positive. Australian women teachers saw distance education as a way of acquiring further qualifications in a profession dominated at the top by men (Evans & Nation, 1993: 272–4). Their vastly poorer sisters in Brazil saw a modest programme of teacher training as one of the few routes to social mobility open to them (Oliveira & Orivel, 1993: 86). We have few hard statistics about the long-term effects of distance education on the lives of students but the odd bits of soft evidence tend to confirm that programmes of part-time education, bent to fit the circumstances of adult students, can be a potent force for social and personal change. This is likely to be true for programmes addressed specifically to teachers as well as for programmes of general education.

The evidence that teacher education at a distance is translated into improved classroom practice is, unfortunately, limited. In some cases it has not been sought. When the Department of Education and Science commissioned the British Open University to get training materials into all secondary schools, it was apparently content to know that they had been distributed and conducted no research on their impact on teachers' behaviour. A small amount of research has been conducted on two of the large-scale programmes in Africa. Two studies in Tanzania looked at the performance of teachers trained at a distance and were able to compare them with those trained face to face (cf. Mählck & Temu, 1989; Chale, 1993). Both studies found that there were few differences in effectiveness between the groups. Students learning at a distance seemed to be at a disadvantage in teaching science (a finding echoed in later studies) and the distance programme was 'relatively less successful in reinforcing self-confidence among female teachers' (Mählck & Temu, 1989: 126). In Zimbabwe limited evidence suggests that teachers trained at a distance were at least as effective as those trained conventionally (Chivore, 1993: 56). In both these cases trainee teachers were deployed in the classroom while they were training so that they inevitably had more classroom practice than their contemporaries who were attending conventional teachers' colleges. We can conclude that the integration of such extensive classroom practice within a centrally organised programme of distance education appears to be effective.

The evidence is more limited than we would like, although it does not compare too badly with what we have on conventional methods of teacher training. It is, perhaps, at its weakest in looking at attitudes and shifts in attitude as teachers are trained, where the data are intriguingly difficult to interpret. Nielsen & Tatto (1993) compared conventional and distance education programmes in Sri Lanka and Indonesia. In Sri Lanka (1993: 113) they found that the distance education programme produced significant positive changes in attitudes among students although there was no significant difference between students at the beginning and end of their courses at conventional colleges. But in Indonesia (op. cit.: 121), in contrast, comparing distance and conventional courses, 'In the realm of attitude acquisition the results were strikingly similar for the two courses: in both, professional attitudes at exit are lower than at entry.' The best working hypothesis may be that factors other than the method of study are at work here.

With all these cautions, and pulling together the evidence from some twelve studies where there are some data on effects, I would conclude that the evidence on effectiveness is sufficiently encouraging for us to argue that distance education can play a legitimate part in teacher education[3]. We can — and should — therefore go on and ask about costs. There are theoretical reasons for expecting distance education to cost less than the conventional alternatives; where teaching materials are prepared in large enough quantities it may be possible to achieve economies of scale that are not open to education with fixed class sizes. But, at the same time, an effective distance education programme requires the commitment of adequate resources for the production of those materials and for the processes of enrolment, administration and tutoring of students. There is no *a priori* reason to assume that any distance education programme will be cost effective.

The empirical evidence is clear:

In ten of the 11 cases [of training teachers at a distance] where data are available, costs for distance education appear to have been lower than the alternative; where we have detailed figures it is reasonable to conclude that distance education programmes can be designed for teachers at a cost of between one-third and two-thirds of conventional programmes (Perraton, 1993: 385).

In part this is because conventional teacher-training is relatively expensive. Even where its curriculum is broadly comparable to that of regular secondary education its costs are often higher. In part it is because some distance-education programmes require students to pay fees, reducing the cost to public budgets, or have opportunity costs that again fall on the student. But, to a large extent, it is because distance education allows for economies of scale and reduces the need to build additional colleges of education and housing for students. By and large distance education programmes for teacher training have run at a large enough scale for these economies to be achieved. They have been achieved despite the relatively heavy, and often crucially important, costs of supervising teaching practice.

Before looking at questions about where we go next, it is worth looking briefly at the methodology of teaching practice, the difficult bit of teacher education. Some programmes have avoided the issue. In the past, as we saw, while some British Open University courses have asked students to undertake and report on classroom work, the University has not organised or supervised classroom practice. In other cases it imposed major logistical demands. In Tanzania:

> District education staff and head teachers were deployed to supervise trainees so that the organisation and supervision of teaching practice was integrated with the work of the regular educational system. In Zimbabwe, where ZINTEC students spent their periods of face-to-face study in four designated colleges, the staff of these colleges were responsible for visiting them in the field, although visits could not, in practice, be made as often as had been planned. . . . The National Teachers' Institute in federal Nigeria had to work with state authorities in providing face-to-face support for teachers. The University of Nairobi had, perhaps, an easier task as it could use the university's own extramural centres for face-to-face study although this still left it with the challenge of liaison with schools and with those responsible for running them.

> Other programmes found that, for one reason or another, it was not possible to visit students in the field and various alternatives were sought. In Nepal distance ruled out visits and it did not prove

possible to arrange teaching practice in schools during the students' face-to-face sessions. Peer-teaching sessions were arranged instead in order to introduce a practical element and a system of resource and satellite schools was established so that groups of teachers from one locality could meet regularly under the guidance of a resource teacher. In Brazil, where LOGOS II did not have the capacity to supervise teaching practice, microteaching was incorporated into face-to-face sessions with teachers (Perraton, 1993: 398).

None of this was particularly easy, not all of it dramatically successful. Many programmes found difficulty in getting the right relationship between educational theory and classroom practice. But, to reiterate, the results do seem to confirm the legitimacy of an approach that combines distance, elements of face-to-face study and supervised teaching practice. The problems in combining the different theoretical and practical elements are shared by all programmes of teacher education whether they are taught conventionally or at a distance.

Where Next?

There are both political and technical questions about what we make of all this. To start with the political ones, it looks as if distance education for teachers is here to stay. There have been over a hundred programmes that have used it for the initial training or the continuing education of teachers. And yet it remains outside the mainstream of teacher education. Ministries of education continue to expand conventional programmes of teacher education and to see distance education as a useful additional technique, appropriate for short-term, or unusual, or marginal purposes but of strictly limited value.

There are perhaps three reasons for this: one good, one bad, one misplaced. The good reason is the assumption that conventional, full-time, education for young adults is a valuable social experience and that, where possible, it is to be preferred to alternatives. The reasoning seems sound provided that our education service also provides opportunities for people who change direction, or decide at the wrong time or in the wrong place, what they really want to do. The bad reason is an automatic assumption that distance education is inferior to conventional education. The misplaced reason is that, as teacher education needs to be grounded in classroom practice, distance education is an inappropriate method for it. Of course, this is right in the sense that we need teachers who are effective in the classroom. And yet the experience of using distance education is that the distance elements can successfully be combined with supervised teaching practice. The logistical difficulties in doing this vary with the scale of the programme but are much the same whether students are alternating their classroom work with study in a teachers' college lecture room or with study from distance-learning materials. Beyond logistics, the difficulties do not lie in the techniques of distance education, but in the planning and running of good classroom practice, raising questions about the relationships between trainee teachers, their mentors, the schools and the colleges that are common to many contemporary discussions of teacher education. And distance education has one great potential advantage here: it opens the possibility of experimenting with different models of teacher education — such as moving closer to an apprenticeship model for example — which may be of benefit at least for some of our students. As the focus and even location of teacher training begins to shift back from the teachers' college to the classroom, with the trainee working alongside a mentor, so there may be a new and enriched role for distance education.

Moving on to the technical, or pedagogical, questions about where we go next may help redress the balance of the paper, which has been over-much about administration. For, despite all the progress it has made, there remains a lot we do not know about the best ways of using distance education. Trenaman (1967) and researchers like Chu & Schramm (1968) set us off with their findings that educational media do not generally differ in their educational effectiveness. You can use most media to teach most subjects. This gives the educational designer or technologist a valuable freedom, to choose media that suit the learner's personal circumstances. That freedom in turn means that institutions have used a variety of media for teaching languages: telephones for oral tutoring at Athabasca, television programmes captured off satellites at the University of Westminster, radio by the BBC and so on. The freedom may not, in practice, always be used to the benefit of students and the choice of media may be over-influenced by the convenience of the administrator rather than of the student. Many programmes of distance education, which start off with grand plans for combining a variety of media, end up dominated by print, offering their students something that is less rich than it might be. And we lack more than a set of heuristics for choosing which medium to use for which purpose, falling back on the obvious like using radio for stimulus and print for a permanent record, or differentiating between the need for immediate and delayed feedback for a particular educational purpose; it would be good to see some progress on something more robust here.

Then there are some more intriguing questions that relate specifically to the teaching of languages at a distance. How, for example, within the bounds of what is practical and economic, can we provide enough practice for a language learner who is not getting to a class or to a language laboratory? (There are limits to the sheer quantity of teaching materials that can be provided to students.) How do we arrange rapid feedback to learners so that they do not learn their mistakes? How do we promote learning at a variety of levels? Distance education lends itself quite well to the lower levels of learning in typologies like Gagné's (1966). In encouraging students to move towards problem-solving, or towards the mastery of generative concepts, we are asking them at the same time to rely on pre-prepared materials and to move on from them into more independent, less predictable, modes of thought. The pedagogical challenge for distance educators is to resolve the dilemma between providing enough support to students to motivate, encourage and help them but not so much that they rely solely on what has been provided. The dilemma may be especially pointed in teaching literature; Lawrence Stenhouse (1975: 82–3) warned us of the danger of trying to reduce, to a simple testable formula, the notion of understanding Hamlet and reminded us that 'Education as induction into knowledge is successful to the extent that it makes the behavioural outcomes of the students unpredictable.' There is a warning here for distance educators seeking behavioural objectives as a planning device. But I wonder whether there is a similar problem about types and levels of learning in learning languages. Are there particular difficulties that arise, because a student is studying much of the time alone, from print or sound or picture, in internalising a rule unfamiliar in the learner's mother tongue so that it becomes natural rather than calculated?

My hunch is that the answers to this kind of question will come from good educational practice generally, and its adaptation to students working at a distance, rather than from a concentration on the differences between distance and conventional education. And so, although in this volume we are concentrating on distance education, our answers may be of wider educational significance. Jerome Bruner (1966: 31) called long ago for, 'a theory of instruction as a guide to pedagogy. . . . that is neutral with regard to ends but exhaustive with regard to means'. Let us hope we can move in that direction — although without too much neutrality about ends.[4]

Notes

1. GCSE: General Certificate of Secondary Education, examination taken by British students when they are about 16.

2. 'A' Levels: Advanced levels, examination taken at 18.
3. Effectiveness data on eight studies are summarised in Perraton (1993: 402-3) and on a further four (Botswana, Kenya, Swaziland, Uganda) in Perraton (1986); cf. also Young *et al.* (1990: 13-22).
4. This paper does not necessarily represent the views of the Commonwealth Secretariat.

References

Avalos, B. (1991) *Approaches to Teacher Education: Initial Teacher Training*. London: Commonwealth Secretariat.
Beeby, C. (1966) *The Quality of Education in Developing Countries*. Cambridge, MA: Harvard University Press.
Bruner, J. (1966) *Toward a Theory of Instruction*. Cambridge, MA: Belknap.
Chale, E. (1993) Tanzania's distance-teaching programme. In Perraton, H. (ed.) (1993): 21–41.
Chivore, B. (1993) The Zimbabwe integrated teacher education course. In Perraton, H. (ed.) (1993): 42–66.
Chu, G. and Schramm, W. (1968) *Learning from Television: What the Research Says*. Stanford: ERIC.
Department for Education. (1992) *Statistical Bulletin* 15/92.
Elvin, H. (1974) The making of the teacher. In *Teacher Education in a Changing Society*. London: Commonwealth Secretariat.
Evans, T. and Nation, D. (1993) Educating teachers at a distance in Australia: some trends. In Perraton, H. (ed.) (1993): 261–86.
Gagné, R. (1966) *The Conditions of Learning*. New York: Holt.
Hawkridge, D., Kinyanjui, P., Nkinyangi, J. and Orivel, F. (1982) In-service teacher education in Kenya. In Perraton, H. (ed.) (1982): 173–213.
Lockheed, M. and Verspoor, A. (1991) *Improving Primary Education in Developing Countries*. Oxford: Oxford University Press.
Mählck, L. and Temu, E. (1989) *Distance Versus College Trained Primary School Teachers: A Case Study from Tanzania*. Paris: International Institute for Educational Planning.
Nielsen, H. and Tatto, M. (1993) Teacher upgrading in Sri Lanka and Indonesia. In Perraton, H. (ed.) (1993): 95–135.
Oliveira, J-B. and Orivel, F. (1993) LOGOS II in Brazil. In Perraton, H. (ed.) (1993): 69–94.
Orwell, G. (1949) *Nineteen Eighty-four.* Harmondsworth: Penguin.
Perraton, H. (ed.) (1982) *Alternative Routes to Formal Education: Distance Teaching for School Equivalency*. Baltimore: Johns Hopkins University Press.
Perraton, H. (1986) *Distance Education: An Economic and Educational Assessment of its Potential for Africa* (Education and training series discussion paper). Washington DC: Education and Training Department, The World Bank.
Perraton, H. (ed.) (1993) *Distance Education for Teacher Training.* London: Routledge.
Prescott, W. and Robinson, B. (1993) Teacher education at the Open University. In Perraton, H. (ed.) (1993): 287–315.
Robinson, B. (1993) The primary teachers' orientation course, Allama Iqbal Open University. In Perraton, H. (ed.) (1993): 228–58.
Schiefelbein, E. and Simmons, J. (1981) *Determinants of School Achievement: A*

Review of Research for Developing Countries. Ottawa: IDRC.

Stenhouse, L. (1975) *An Introduction to Curriculum Research and Development.* London: Heinemann.

Trenaman, J. (1967) *Communication and Comprehension.* London: Longman.

Wittgenstein, L. (1922) *Tractatus Logico-Philosophicus.* Translated by C. K. Ogden. London: Routledge and Kegan Paul.

Young, M., Perraton, H., Jenkins, J., and Dodds, T. (1990) *Distance Teaching for the Third World: the Lion and the Clockwork Mouse* (2nd ed). Cambridge: International Extension College.

3 Language Teacher Training by Distance Learning: Models of Delivery

ROBERT LEACH

Introduction

A notional language teacher training syllabus would include modules on each of the four language skills, on phonology, on language acquisition, on language analysis, on methodology, on classroom management, on use of materials and media, and on principles of pedagogy (see Figure 3.1).

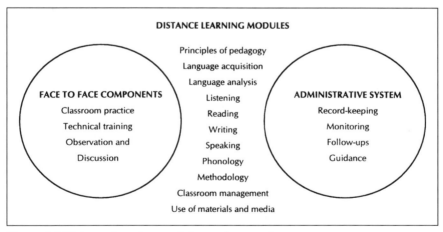

DISTANCE LEARNING MODULES

Principles of pedagogy
Language acquisition
Language analysis

FACE TO FACE COMPONENTS

Classroom practice
Technical training
Observation and
Discussion

Listening
Reading
Writing
Speaking
Phonology

ADMINISTRATIVE SYSTEM

Record-keeping
Monitoring
Follow-ups
Guidance

Methodology
Classroom management
Use of materials and media

Figure 3.1 Distance learning modules and support

As Figure 3.1 suggests, the central pillar of distance modules needs to be buttressed by face-to-face support and, equally importantly, by an administrative system. However good your modules and your tutoring, if you do not have an effective administrative system then the pillar cannot stand. Face-to-face teaching, oddly enough, can often manage to stagger on in the most appalling administrative conditions. But distance learning can't. This paper will describe models of administration, in the context of how the distance-learning mode can benefit learner, tutor and system.

First, however, I would like to highlight, perhaps with some productive complementarity with other contributions to this volume, the *educational* advantages of distance learning for training language teachers.

The type of syllabus illustrated in Figure 3.1 would feed into classroom observation and supervised teaching practice, and might also involve training in the target language. These additional items would involve face-to-face tuition, although Holmberg (1985) and Oxford (1993) have shown the potential for language learning by distance methods. For the main syllabus content, however, it can be argued that distance learning can not only deliver the skills and knowledge to support the necessarily practical face-to-face training, but can also do so in ways that are of particular value to the trainee language teacher.

Perhaps the highest on the agenda of these is the idea of learner autonomy, which is more obvious in distance learning than any other mode, perhaps even more than in self-study. Awareness of one's own learning is probably greater in distance learning than in self-study because the positive feedback from the tutor enhances this awareness, while the learning of self-study may seem more natural, and more unconscious. Self-esteem as an autonomous learner needs to be established and reinforced by feedback. In face-to-face teaching the passive and directed side of learning can be over-emphasised, but in distance learning *de facto* the learner is in charge. The trainee teacher's self-respect in this regard can be a precursor to the new teacher's respect for the learner and desire to foster the learner's self-directed learning. The implications are very powerful, and they are essential in distance learning but not in face-to-face, where teacher autocracy is still very common.

Another important element of good distance learning is the provision of high quality learning materials that are self-explanatory and that are couched in language accessible to the learner. Learning by example, the trainee teacher can see that the good qualities in the materials on the course can be copied in their own teaching, in developing new materials and in good blackboard/OHP practice. These qualities include good layout, use of headings, clarity of instructions, good contextualisation, referral back to previous learning, clear learning aims, summarisation and review, and consistency of style and presentation.

The example in Appendix 3.1, the first page from a teacher-training resource, exemplifies some of these features: minimal number of words on the page, plenty of white space, bulleted list, clear hierarchy of headings, simple introduction and aims couched in measurable terms.

The resource pack illustrated in Appendix 3.1 is used to prepare language and other tutors to teach in Further and Adult Education for the City and Guilds 7305 qualification, often used as the first year of a Certificate in Education. It attempts to give good general messages about materials design, but more than this to demonstrate with a simple set of contents and aims good educational practice.

Each section of the resource includes aims, activities, group activities (for study groups or face-to-face teaching), case studies, examples (shorter than case studies), checklists and action plans.

All of these features help to stimulate the development of a good teacher, and with the exception of the group activities are inherent features of good distance learning. The constraints of the distance-learning model are in fact imposing a greater need for good practice. As I am sure all language teachers would agree, the *language* teacher is more focused on process than the average teacher of the average subject, and thus has more opportunity to develop good awareness of and contribution to the learning process. While the necessarily good quality materials of the distance-learning course impose a discipline of excellence on the materials, the distance learner's relative isolation can help to foster a discipline of learning awareness. Distance can be made to work for the learner almost in a metaphorical way: distance learning can help to create a *distancing* between learner and what is learnt, a more self-reflective mentality often lost in the more busy and pressured atmosphere of much classroom-based training. This reflectiveness can be exemplified in another page from *Teaching and Training Adults*, which asks the learner to reflect on learning up to now and to plan the next stage (Appendix 3.2).

Though such a worksheet could well be used in a face-to-face context, it is possibly more likely to be filled in with thought and attention if it is the only means of developing awareness than if the trainee teacher has peers and tutors to do the reflecting for him or her.

All the above features of materials and the foregrounding of learner autonomy as an aim both for trainee teacher and for language learner should help to encourage a teacher towards a new awareness of learning process, of counselling, of the need for learning strategies, of the importance of learner-centred materials, of the role of assessment and monitoring, and of the role of evaluation in any course being taught or studied. Syllabus planning and methodology are also obviously central to any type of course, and the ideas behind them can be presented well by an imaginative distance-learning approach.

It is not intended that the above discussion constitutes a defence of distance learning at the expense of other teacher-training methods; that would create an absurd and over-abstract contrast. It is certainly true that many things can be taught either way and, as Hilary Perraton (Chapter 2) says, through different media, and for language teachers it is unquestionable that some things cannot be taught at a distance. What the experience of the National Extension College (NEC) has shown us, however, is that many of the features of distance learning can be very beneficial.

I hope that this emphasis on the learner as central actor in the teacher-training process provides a context for looking at practical models of distance learning for language teachers. However, it is also worth prefacing the description of these models with a note on the assessment mechanisms involved. Teacher training courses may be assessed by a combination of three elements: supervised teaching experience; written examination; and coursework projects. There are, in addition, modular and competence-based courses, which have different patterns of assessment, but I cannot pretend that distance delivery of this type of competence assessment is far enough advanced for me to be able to comment on it at this stage. Instead, I will present three actual systems that NEC uses and that are assessed by coursework, by portfolio, by practical tests and by written examinations. In one case these are synthesised, under a model pioneered by BTEC[1] and currently being developed for GNVQs[2] to provide an integrated assessment of core skills as well as discrete elements.

After the contrasting features of these current existing systems have been presented, I will outline a possible model that we hope to develop with the Bell Educational Trust and the London University Institute of Education, but the assessment mechanisms for this have yet to be established.

The main focus of my description will be on the administrative aspects of these courses, but I hope that the way I deal with this topic will also remind you of the opportunities that distance learning gives for the sorts of skills development outlined above, for assessment, and for support and guidance, choice and feedback to students.

Three Administrative Models for Distance Learning

GCSEs[3] and 'A' levels[4]

The first model (Figure 3.2) is the standard model for the majority of NEC's distance courses. It is relatively cheap, costing about £170 for a GCSE course including the authentication or assessment of coursework for accreditation. This cost covers a set of course materials in a ringbinder, now including an audio cassette, which introduces the course and provides a selection of encouraging statements by past students. It also covers tutor-marked assignments, some of which relate to coursework assessment, which I will describe in a moment, and occasionally there are computer-marked assignments as well. Face-to-face study weekends are charged extra. A typical cost of a weekend English GCSE or 'A' level study weekend would be £90.

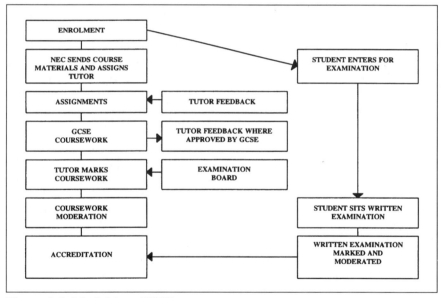

Figure 3.2 Model 1 — GCSEs

This distance model is used for a wide range of general and vocational qualifications and for leisure courses. It allows students to take a wide range of courses and to have contact with tutors through the marking of assignments and use of comment sheets and query cards. Each course is written to include up to 16 assignments (though more can be requested by students who feel they need more practice). The courses include study guides and, for examined courses, revision guides as well as teaching materials divided up into units, which may cover two to eight hours' study time. Many courses have a modular structure, which allows some choice of coverage as well as opportunities to pause if a break in studies is required. Each enrolment is valid for up to three years, but there is no time limit for the completion of individual assignments. Thus there is flexibility, although tutors and students can agree a series of deadlines for assignment completion, which may help to create a fruitful pattern of study. Telephone contact is encouraged.

To actually obtain the GCSE qualification, students must register individually with the examination board, submit the coursework and sit the exam at a local centre. This assessment opportunity is, incidentally, now under threat.

The general NEC system first enrols the student after a diagnostic process and automatically assigns a tutor, if possible in the student's region of the UK. Overseas students are assigned a UK-based tutor at random. The tutor then writes an introductory letter or makes a phone call, and the student receives a biography of the tutor, a set of course materials, and a set of about 15 assignment forms in triplicate, which are used to monitor their progress administratively and academically. Tutors are paid by the completed and marked assignment, plus expenses for postage, stationery, telephone calls and other essential expenses such as the purchase of set books.

The student receives a student book and an exam book as well as the course package, which itself contains a study guide, an assignment guide and the learning materials. The student studies the first units, and sends the first assignment to the tutor with the first assignment form. This identifies the student, course, assignment and tutor, and has a blank space for the tutor's overall comment on a script and grade. The script itself, and the top copy of the form, are returned to the student (though they are requested by our learner support department for random monitoring from time to time). A second copy of the form is returned to NEC, and the tutor retains the third copy. The NEC copy of the form is used to record the grade given on a database and to trigger payment for the tutor.

This process continues throughout the course as all the assignments are done. Meanwhile, the student enters for the examination and usually prepares coursework. This can be an investigation into mathematical relationships, a sociological survey or a creative and literary piece. In most cases the plan and perhaps a draft of the coursework are seen and commented on by the tutor, but the final draft is merely 'authenticated' as the candidate's own work by the tutor and marked by the examination board. When the course assignments are finished, the student receives a course completion certificate from NEC, and sits the final written examination.

Before and during the course, the student has the chance to phone NEC, or the tutor, or write to or visit an independent guidance service, to discuss progress, progression routes and examination chances. NEC helps with the administrative requirements for exam entry, but we deliberately ask students to make their own direct requests to the examination board for syllabuses and past papers. About 15,000 students enrol with NEC in a year and follow the procedure in this model.

Technician Training Scheme (TTS)

The second model (Figure 3.3) is more complex, and involves close liaison by NEC with both employers and local face-to-face colleges. The accreditation is by BTEC (or SCOTVEC[5] in Scotland), which means that there is separate unit accreditation but that a set of units can comprise a BTEC National Diploma provided that core skills are also assessed. This model depends on the co-operation of local colleges who choose and provide most of the tutors, while NEC provides the course materials including electronic kits and basic computers or, increasingly, computer simulations of them. Core skills are assessed by a combination of workplace evidence and evidence from assignments.

In model 3.2, students follow a course over a period corresponding to the UK's conventional academic year from September to June. They must attend college on three to four occasions to sit tests and receive instruction, which in the end lead to unit credits in various areas of telecommunications and other fields of electronic engineering. The scheme is attractive to employers as it allows employees to train while continuing to work full-time and it has a low drop-out and failure rate. Of 1,200 students in 1989, for example, 85% passed and 45% achieved a Merit. Though numbers declined through to 1992, the proportions of awards remained constant.

Employer sponsorship means that students are not financially responsible for their course, but does encourage a high success rate, probably because it is tied to career progression. The 'lock-step' September to June programme lacks flexibility, but motivates students to complete work in a reasonable period and in a regular pattern.

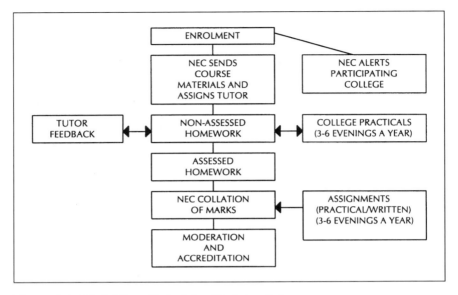

Figure 3.3 Model 2 — Technician Training Scheme

While the college is responsible for tutoring and marking, NEC is responsible for tracking students through the various units of the certificate, collecting marks, and arranging for all student work to be collated at NEC for an annual BTEC Moderator visit. The cost is nevertheless reasonable, at £225 per unit. NEC pays participating colleges a fee per student unit, and the colleges pay the tutor on the normal payroll. Each course in this scheme has a different combination of assessed and non-assessed homework, phase tests and end tests, distance and face-to-face study, but the overall attendance at college per year varies between zero attendance (for some theoretical courses assessed at a distance) to the more usual three to six evenings of tuition and three to six of assessment. Some colleges also offer weekend facilities. There are various numbers of assignments per course, but ten is an average over an academic year from September to June. The assessment material is written afresh every year, at a cost of £5–10,000 for a range of assessments for 20 courses. It has been suggested that we move towards an assessment bank, with different combinations of questions chosen each year, but the technical nature of the courses and the fast-changing technology have so far prevented this. Some assessments are purely practical — such as demonstrating proficiency with an ammeter or an oscilloscope — but most include a paper-and-pen element. A complex averaging formula is followed at the end of the year to award final marks. Because the colleges currently follow academic years, enrolments only take place in September and January, although all other NEC courses enrol at any time. TTS enrolments have declined recently from 1,300 to 500 a year, due to redundancies in British Telecom and a less sympathetic training culture in the industry generally.

Degree and Professional Studies (DPS)

A third model (Figure 3.4), the Degree and Professional Study Scheme, is on the other hand increasing rapidly, mainly because London University has recently offered new syllabuses in a number of popular subjects. This model, unlike the others, does not offer any course materials, although this is under review. Instead, students are referred by London University or other awarding bodies, the Engineering Council and the Institute of Linguists, for tutorial support as they work towards degrees and diplomas. The tutors themselves set work in conjunction with the students, and all returned work is sent via NEC so that we can monitor tutors' responses fully. These students are asked to pay a registration fee of £120, which includes one free assignment. There is normally a different tutor for each paper of the degree or diploma, and tutors set work and mark it on receipt of an assignment card from the student. If the student wants more work set and marked, more assignment cards are purchased on a sale or return basis at £20 each. Typically a student might complete six assignments in a year, but many work mainly by self-study and may submit only a few assignments each year as they work towards a degree over six to eight years. Most students, however, are on shorter Institute of Linguists courses, which are offered in a number of languages.

The Degree and Professional Study Scheme is a direct private study operation that is popular with students at undergraduate and, primarily, post-graduate level. The model relies more upon the educational planning, delivery and assessment designing skills of the tutors than is the case with conventional open learning, which may be largely materials based. The personal rapport between student and tutor is very important, as there are no specific course materials and it is up to tutors to recommend books and periodicals and to set suitable assignments. The range of courses includes the nine languages to postgraduate Institute of Linguists levels, a number of postgraduate engineering diplomas, and external degrees from London University. We are soon to offer support for the Institute of Linguists Diploma in English for International Communication, and for the London Advanced Diploma in Education, which will have a new delivery model.

- Enrolment

- Registration and assignment card

- Tutor sets first assignment

- Student submits work and tutor marks it

- Student buys set of 5 or 10 assignment cards

- Student is set work. Submits it and receives feedback as required

- Unused assignment cards returned to NEC

- Student sits examinations in each paper when ready

Figure 3.4 Model 3 — Degree and Professional Studies

The current DPS system allows for maximum flexibility as students may decide to do as many assignments as they like, as often as they like, and complete the assignments in a way that suits the student after discussion with the tutor. Results, from the Institute of Linguists in particular, are excellent, and 90% marks in examination papers are not uncommon. It is recognised that these results reflect the excellence of the tutors and the high motivation of students. A weakness is that, as the system relies entirely on the tutor's choice of materials, the student has no other academic resource. By contrast, NEC's main distance education system relies heavily on carefully prepared course materials, thus releasing tutors to concentrate on marking assignments rather than setting study programmes and tasks as well. In this sense, students may be more likely to become disaffected and abandon a programme of study in the DPS system than in the main system if they lose confidence in their tutor. On the other hand, it is always possible to change tutors in either system.

These models have been generated by a combination of learner needs, provider needs and, in the case of the Technician Training Scheme (model 2), sponsor needs. In general it is difficult to identify which needs are most important. It would probably be fair to say that where a learner need is perceived, it can lead to a new model of open learning.

All the models share features that are designed to empower learners and reduce disaffection. In a recent paper (Leach & Webb, 1993), we describe students' perceptions of one model, together with their aims, social and educational position, and achievements in their open learning courses. In conclusion, we offer suggestions on how disaffection is challenged and often overcome.

Language Teacher Training

The three models above represent contrasting approaches to the provision of relatively low-cost support for students almost entirely by distance learning. A fourth model, which we are developing for language teacher trainees with both the Institute of Education in London and the Bell Educational Trust in Cambridge, is based on a combination of all three models.

The aim is to produce a modular form of delivery that can be flexible enough to provide relevant teaching and support for a range of needs: for the pre-experience native-speaker teacher of adults or the post-experience overseas second-language speaker teacher of primary age children, with extra modules for special purposes and for training in the grammar and other aspects of the target language, in socio- and psycholinguistics, and in other areas.

Initial planning has used a set of four assignments as the unit of delivery, which matches the current pattern of the Institute of Education Advanced Diploma in Education. Course materials are currently provided by the Institute, but NEC intends to develop its own. For post-experience students, the majority of the delivery will be by distance learning, with a face-to-face element at the end. For an experimental period, the cost of a package of four assignments will be £50, partly subsidised by London University. For the Bell version of the model, each module will be self-standing, and the course will be open to pre-experience as well as post-experience trainees, although there will always be a face-to-face and teaching practice component before a pre-experience award is offered. It is expected that a modular TEFL diploma will be developed in parallel with the course, the accreditation offered in the first instance jointly by Bell and NEC, but later by other awarding bodies.

The success of this approach for language-teacher training is yet to be evaluated, but the other models are sufficiently well-established for any institution offering relatively large-scale, distance learning language-teacher training to take them on. There are, as in all course models, polarities that need to be considered. Do you want to be prescriptive, as in the GCSE model, or unconstrained by materials, as in the DPS model? Should you send the materials all at once, or in modules? What guidance points are needed for the trainee? Between units, as in TTS? Throughout the course, as in GCSE? On student demand, as in DPS? How frequent should tutor intervention be? How proactive, how reactive? What forms of assessment are suitable? These are perennial questions for all distance learning, but the models I have described do at least provide concrete examples of living, current practice.

I would like to finish with a case study of a distance-learning language-teaching MA that I never finished, at an anonymous institution.

I registered in March 1989, and heard nothing until October, when I received a badly duplicated set of materials designed to teach me how to teach reading skills. They were difficult to read, in all ways, but I did realise that no feedback was required until the following April and therefore was not motivated to study them at all. I received no personal communication until well into the course, but was finally given the name of a tutor. In January I received another badly duplicated set of materials on writing skills. It contained nothing about academic writing, my current interest, so I wrote to ask for a reading list. I was sent an apology that no relevant books were known to my tutor. Finally, in March 1990 I received a badly duplicated set of materials about listening skills. At that point I gave up, wrote a letter to explain why, and received no reply. . . .

I hope that we can all do better than I did, and than they did.

Notes

1.   BTEC: Business and Technology Education Council.
2.   GNVQ: General National Vocational Qualification.
3.   GCSE: General Certificate of Secondary Education, examination taken at about 16.
4.   'A' levels: Advanced level, examination taken at about 18.
5.   SCOTVEC: Scottish Vocational Educational Council.

References

Calder, J. (ed.) (1993) *Disaffection and Diversity: Overcoming Barriers for Adult Learners.* London: Falmer Press.
Holmberg, B. (1985) Teaching foreign languages at a distance. *Distance Education* 6(1), 79–90.
Leach, R. and Webb, R. (1993) Opportunities through Open Learning. In Calder, J. (ed.) (1993): 91–109.
NEC. (1991) *Teaching and Training Adults.* NEC.
NEC. (1992) *A New Way to Learn.* NEC.
NEC. (1992) *A New Way to Train.* NEC.
Oxford, R. (1993) Factors affecting achievement in a satellite-delivered Japanese language program. *American Journal of Distance Education* 7(1), 11–25.

Appendix 3.1

TEACHING ADULTS

Section 1: You as a tutor

You have already experienced being a learner and are now thinking about what it means to be a tutor. As a first step you need to consider what being a teacher involves, both in general and in your own particular case.

Contents

The topics covered in this section are as follows:

The qualities of a good tutor

Your role as a tutor

What are you expected to teach?

Observing tutors at work

Keeping a personal development log.

AIMS

When you have completed this section you should be able to:

▼ *describe the qualities of a good tutor*

▼ *write a description of your own teaching role*

▼ *identify what you are expected to teach*

▼ *observe other tutors teaching in a systematic way*

▼ *begin the process of self-evaluation*

▼ *keep a personal development log.*

Appendix 3.2

Teaching adults

 ACTION PLAN

Now that you have completed this section, use the following sheet to:
▼ review your achievement of the aims listed at the start
▼ plan any further learning.

Objective	Achieved: Fully	Almost	Partly	Not at all
Describe the qualities of a good teacher	☐	☐	☐	☐
Write a description of your own teaching role	☐	☐	☐	☐
Identify what you are expected to teach	☐	☐	☐	☐
Observe other teachers' teaching in a systematic way	☐	☐	☐	☐
Begin the process of self-evaluation	☐	☐	☐	☐
Keep a personal development log	☐	☐	☐	☐

Now review those outcomes you have not fully met and note down against each one the action you will now take.

I need to find out more about:

I need to develop my skills in:

I will need access to the following resources:

I will need the help of the following people:

I will plan my further learning by:
Outcome   Date

I will achieve my outcomes by:
Outcome   Date

4 'You Are Your Own Best Resource': Promoting Confidence and Autonomous Learning in Teacher Education at a Distance — a Case Study

ELSPETH BROADY

Introduction

Michael Wallace's 'reflective' model of professional education claims that professional competence is built up from *received knowledge*, that is, the 'concepts, research findings, theories and skills which are widely accepted as part of the necessary intellectual content of the profession' and *experiential knowledge*, the knowledge derived from practice. Both of these sources of knowledge then inform practice, but it is reflection on practice that allows for the development and extension of professional competence (Wallace, 1991: 14–15).

This chapter looks at some of the difficulties that arose in promoting an effective balance between received knowledge, experiential knowledge and reflection on a distance teacher education course for modern languages' tutors working in British adult education. In particular, I wish to examine how participants' anxieties, exacerbated by the isolation and an apparent emphasis on learning from print that distance learning can imply, led them to focus particularly strongly on the 'received knowledge' part of the model and downplay, at least initially, the confident exploration of their own experience. I suggest that the regular discussions with tutors and peers that are available on face-to-face courses constitute an important means of restoring this balance. It is often in talking about teaching with peers 'in the same boat' that student teachers gain confidence in experimenting and reflecting on new ideas: things that work can be passed on, while problems can be shared. The greatest challenge to teacher education at a distance, then, is to find other ways of stimulating this kind of exchange.

The case study that follows examines participants' perceptions of their learning as well as my own reflections as a course tutor. The analysis here is 'pre-scientific' and impressionistic, since the data informing the study — course evaluation questionnaires and participants' retrospective accounts of their learning, produced as part of a personal portfolio — were generated for other purposes. Since I also attempt to interpret others' experience, as well as my own, it is necessarily speculative. However, beyond these limitations, my intention is to explore some of the difficulties that arose on one distance teacher education course in the hope that this will shed interesting light on the challenges faced by student teachers and teacher educators working at a distance. In the final section of this paper, I suggest some approaches for meeting those challenges.

The Course

The RSA Diploma in Teaching Foreign Languages to Adults (RSA Dip. TFLA) is a post-experience diploma for practising modern-language teachers in adult, further and higher education. The Language Centre at Brighton Polytechnic had successfully run a face-to-face course leading to this diploma in the early eighties. The decision to offer a distance-learning version came in 1990 when we were invited by the Institute for Applied Language Studies, University of Edinburgh to become a local centre for their print-based course.[1] As a local centre, we became responsible for recruiting participants within an approximate catchment area of 80 miles, for all aspects of course assessment, and for the forty hours of face-to-face workshops. We ran the course twice between 1990 and 1992, each time with thirteen participants.

The course was designed for practising teachers with a minimum of two years' teaching experience and offered the possibility of updating teaching skills and obtaining a teaching qualification. The explicitly stated objectives for the distance-learning version of the RSA Dip. TFLA were as follows:

- to develop a critical understanding of the objectives of language teaching;
- to acquire a knowledge of the means through which these objectives may be achieved;
- to develop the skills necessary for the effective organisation of adult language learning.

Participants were recruited mainly from further and adult education, but a minority were teaching in higher education or private language schools. As shown in the Outline Course Programme for 1991–92 (Appendix 4.1), the course ran over ten months from September to July and consisted of six distance learning booklets, with one weekend workshop per term. Assessed course work was made up of seven tasks, typically short essays or reports; two assignments, which were longer pieces of work involving more personal research; a teaching manual covering ten hours' teaching; and a Personal Portfolio, comprising five personally selected written pieces reflecting professional development over the year. Assessment of practical teaching was made formatively by four visits from a local 'mentor' and summatively by two visits from course tutors and, if necessary, a further visit by an RSA Moderator.

The Effects of Anxiety

> Over-anxious adult learners tend not to trust themselves and thus turn to authority for guidance. . . (anxiety) tends to interfere with and inhibit original thought. Tasks requiring some degree of personal judgement are thus harder for the over-anxious student participant than tasks demanding self-critical conformity to rules (Rogers, 1986: 164).

From my perspective as course tutor, Rogers' comments accurately characterise the process that participants on the RSA Dip. TFLA seemed to experience and that had an impact on the way they approached their work at a distance and their expectations relating to the workshops.

Initial anxieties tended to focus on the amount of reading involved in working through course booklets and recommended reading, and on producing written work. Frustration and confusion was expressed about what was perceived as 'jargon' and 'theory', despite an explicit attempt to deal with these predictable concerns in the introductory booklet. Up until then, participants had seen teaching as something they 'did' rather than 'read about' or 'analysed'. They suddenly found themselves on a print-based distance course having to do a lot of reading and analysing. Uncertainty about how to relate this 'received knowledge' to 'experiential knowledge' and practice seemed to lead, on the one hand, to a rejection of the value of the literature altogether and, on the other hand, to a search in the literature for prescriptions — and a concomitant undervaluing of personal expertise. This in turn tended to result in bland, judgmental written work with little reference to personal practice, and practical teaching that was constrained and unresponsive. As one participant commented in her learner diary after an observation:

> I knew there had been something wrong with the class . . . I was using too many theoretical techniques and putting myself and my students into a straight-jacket [sic]. I didn't have enough confidence in myself or my students. In the one and a half hours, I wanted, as usual, the lesson to go just as planned, controlled by theories of what should and shouldn't be done.

In this quote the participant reveals her awareness of the dangers implicit in over-emphasising 'received knowledge'. However, with little opportunity to discuss their own teaching experiences week to week, participants were not able to reflect interactively on what they were reading, and thus to place it in some kind of perspective.

In the same way, some participants tended to develop an over-critical attitude to their own teaching, leading to crises of confidence, as illustrated by the following quote from one participant's portfolio:

> While I felt excitement at the beginning, and was able to take on board new ideas and consolidate new skills, around the middle of the year, I experienced a period where I felt that everything was going wrong. I had too many different things to consider when preparing and teaching, so that these became too analytical and conscious. Lessons were taking me longer to prepare because I was questioning every item I included: why is this useful, what function does it perform, is it necessary, would another item do better? In teaching I worried about whether I was correcting appropriately, whether my explanations were clear and necessary, whether there was enough variety, communication etc. . .

While such loss of confidence through what we might see as *too much* reflection seems to me to be symptomatic of a rich learning process, the process is potentially demotivating when there is no forum for regular discussion with peers.

In an ideal world, it might have been assumed that as practising teachers, these participants would have around them a circle of colleagues with whom to discuss their experiences. However, adult-education tutors typically work in the evenings, with little contact with other tutors. Furthermore, staff development opportunities in this sector tend to be limited. In only five cases out of twenty six was any contribution made by an employer towards a participant's course fees; in only four cases did participants benefit from any other training opportunities offered by their institution or education authority. The local mentor scheme had originally been designed to ensure local support for participants. However, we discovered that in the majority of cases the local mentor's contribution was strictly limited to observation visits. This is hardly surprising since there was no paid contractual agreement between the mentor and the study centre. Participants were often hesitant therefore about making any further demands on the mentor's time.

External Standards

As the course continued, participants' worries started to focus on external standards. While I, in my role as course tutor, stressed the importance of exploration and experimentation, the participants were keenly aware that working towards an RSA Diploma implied that their performance would be judged against a set of externally defined criteria. While every attempt was made to make these criteria clear in the course documents — task and assignment guidelines were clearly stated in a separate course booklet — their exact interpretation became one of the participants' prime concerns at workshops. In fact, briefing participants for assessed written work at the workshops was for me one of the most problematic aspects of course management. In response to repeated demands for explication, I ended up in the role of 'answer person' (Curran, 1976) making detailed suggestions as to how to go about assessed tasks, almost to the extent of providing a model answer.

Trying to meet this expressed need for clarification placed considerable pressure on workshop time, time needed to devote to precisely those activities, such as micro-teaching and small group discussions, that would promote the sharing of judgments and experiences that might alleviate the anxiety! On the feed-back questionnaires, which participants filled in after each workshop, the two most frequent responses to the question 'What would you have liked to spend more time on during this workshop?' were: (1) briefing for assessed tasks and assignments and (2) sharing experiences with colleagues. My impression after every workshop was that we had done nothing else — but there never seemed to be enough time.

The Role of the Workshops

In retrospect, I think this points to a crucial dilemma: so much of what the participants felt they needed to spur their confidence as teachers derived most easily from the face-to-face workshops, rather than from the distance-learning materials. It was the workshops that provided support and reassurance, and through experiential learning such as micro-teaching, the stimulus to go back into the classroom and try out new ideas, as the following quotes from participants' questionnaires and learner diaries suggest:

> The workshops provided contact, friendship and fellow-feeling. . . . Perhaps one of the most useful things to come out of these weekends was what we learnt from each other. . . . Sharing of knowledge and experiences from very different teaching situations shed new light on our own experiences and led to questioning and reappraisal.

> It was at this point (January) that general panic seemed to set in for the first time, as I really was very unsure as to what the next tasks expected of me. Fortunately, this coincided with the second workshop. This was bliss! I was not the only one being confused! In fact there were some struggling even more. What a relief! The one disadvantage of distance learning is, of course, that it is a lonely path to take. The weekend workshops did therefore help tremendously. Through discussion, tasks 3–6 suddenly 'fell into place' and I walked away from that workshop with my self-confidence restored!

> (The workshop was) useful — having the course explained and meeting the tutors, so it's no longer quite a mammoth and frightening task.

> Very useful — interchange of ideas, tips, practices with the other students, particularly to throw light on what you are doing yourself.

> Micro-teaching was an especially valuable element of the latter two workshops.

> Experiencing trial Dutch lessons and a session of communicative activities were a priceless experience and have since been made use of.

Yet, of course, the workshops accounted for only a small proportion of the total study time required by the course: the bulk of the learning was, at least in theory, to be carried by the printed materials, backed up by further reading and given focus by written course work. Particularly in the first half of the course, it almost felt as though the participants had rejected the whole notion of distance learning and saw the workshops as representing the 'real' learning. Contrary to my expectations that distance learning would favour autonomous learning on the part of the participants, it seemed to be doing the opposite as they saw clarification and explanation in Brighton as the vital 'fix' that would enable them to continue. In reaction to participant anxiety and under time pressure, it was all too easy for me to slip into a 'telling-them-how-to-do-it' mode in order to try and forestall panic and consternation.

An Instrumental View of Learning

Providing for distance learning of any kind obliges us to ask questions about learning efficiency. Distance learning may offer flexibility in terms of when and where study takes place, but it puts the onus on participants to fit their learning time in with competing demands. The convenient 'window of time' represented by the weekly course meeting is not available, nor is the (relatively) convenient access to learning resources implied by regular attendance at an educational institution. Given such constraints, it was hardly surprising that participants on the RSA Dip. TFLA sometimes took a very instrumental view of their learning — the 'you tell me what to do and I'll do it' approach — and called for highly structured input and tightly specified output. This gave rise to another dilemma for me as course tutor. On the one hand, I was concerned to encourage exploration and reflection: on the other, to minimise confusion and maximise positive study time. Let me illustrate this dilemma with reference to participant reactions to a key learning tool, the Course Bibliographies. These were produced by the local centres and in our case, consisted of a preliminary bibliography of six key books that participants were encouraged to buy, and a supplementary bibliography of around thirty titles, organised by topic with indications of the relevance of each book for particular written assignments. The guidelines made it clear that participants were not expected to read every book, but should aim to at least 'dip' into one book per topic. However, even with this proviso, the bibliography emerged on both years as a source of dissatisfaction:

> The list of books seems to be endless and very discouraging.

> Necessary reading only should be mentioned. Only add other titles if really compulsory.

These comments point to another difference in perspective that emerged between the participants and myself. I had conceived of the bibliography as a 'resource', encouraging the participants to look at several works in order to find the one that best suited their interests. The participants saw it as a list of obligatory reading, which, given its length, was confusing and threatening.

The dilemma of how to present a bibliography as a useful learning tool is illustrated most pertinently in the following comments from one of the participants:

> One of the most discouraging points of the course must have been the incredibly vast and never-ending list of books to be read: whenever I spent money on one, I seemed to turn a page in a workbook to find yet another 'list for further reading'. There was a lot of reading to be done. This seemed to be the main point raised at the first workshop, that people wanted the information for each task set out more clearly and in order. I tended to agree at first, but the more I thought about, and the further I progressed in the course, I felt that it was much more rewarding and gave me a better sense of achievement having gathered all the necessary information myself from all the sources recommended. I had been given the freedom of choice and it made the whole course more challenging. Had it all been presented in the course material in order of tasks and only with information relevant to each task, as people had wanted, I would have felt that I had merely completed a course of material summary instead of research. I certainly would not have been able to learn as much and to form my own opinions and ideas about as many subjects as I did.

In this particular case, then, a learning tool designed to offer the participant a range of possibilities stimulated a more autonomous approach to work. It must be pointed out, however, that this participant lived near the Language Centre and was able to travel fairly easily to our library. For a participant living some 60 miles away from the local centre, the 'resource' approach was often unhelpful. Without the opportunity to browse through the books recommended, no real choice could be made: in fact, a whole afternoon of precious study time could be spent simply trying to track down three titles, where one might have sufficed. Stephen Kemmis' concept of 'inauthentic labour' is relevant here. He uses it to describe how computers can play a key role in learning by reducing unnecessary work, such as re-typing and calculation, thus freeing up the learner for more relevant work (cited by Higgins, 1988: 40). The danger, I realised, of setting up work that was too open-ended, or demanded resources participants did not easily have available, was to engage them in 'inauthentic labour', with a resultant waste of energy. As one participant commented on the drawbacks of distance learning: 'It is possible to over and/or under work on a course like this and get insecure/demotivated/lost.'

In response to calls for more carefully structured input and guidance, I distributed at one workshop a Study Guide (see Appendix 4.2), breaking down the forthcoming work into steps, a technique reminiscent of Open University distance-learning materials. This was very positively received and it made me reflect that perhaps highly explicit guidance of this kind can help to promote confidence and allow participants to feel that the work set is manageable. There is always a chance of encouraging thus a narrow, uniform approach to the work, but as John Higgins comments: 'Making learning difficult does not make it more valuable. Making learning convenient does, in general, increase the amount of it that takes place' (Higgins, 1988: 41). Nevertheless, this does not solve the dilemma that by managing participants' learning for them, the teacher educator may be closing down opportunities for participants to explore vital learning skills, of value to them both as learners and teachers.

Let me summarise, then, some of the difficulties we experienced in Brighton on the RSA Dip. TFLA course. The participants, faced with reflecting about teaching primarily from written material tended to look for prescriptions as a means of finding their way through 'the theory'. At first, they did not feel very confident about developing their own ideas about teaching in written form and analysing their own practice in a balanced way. They were uncertain as to how to use the professional literature. Their isolation from each other and from other professionals tended to exacerbate these difficulties. There was not sufficient time at the workshops to adequately resolve them and it was easy to fall into the trap of providing answers, rather than providing the circumstances for participants to develop their own insights and at the same time, share problems.

As course tutor, I discovered that I had made two naive assumptions: that practising teachers would feel confident about their 'feel' for what worked and what didn't in the classroom and would thus approach reflecting on teaching through reading and written work with equanimity; and that participants would have easy access to local mentors and colleagues for support and guidance. I also failed to foresee that the very fact of returning to study would be likely to make a number of participants question their own expertise and ascribe to course tutors the role of sole experts. One of my important tasks as course tutor was to encourage them to see that within their own classrooms and their own institutions were learning opportunities of greater value than the books in the Brighton Polytechnic Library!

Addressing the Problem

What our experience makes clear is the importance of helping student teachers discover how received knowledge, experiential knowledge and reflection on practice interact to promote professional competence. This is true of any teacher education course, but perhaps more crucial on a distance-learning course where there is less chance for mediation between received and experiential knowledge through peer exchange. What is also clear is the importance of helping participants understand what distance learning involves. In the light of some of the problems we experienced, I identified the following goals for our development of the course:

(1)   to encourage the participants to focus first and foremost on what actually happens in real classrooms — their own and those of fellow teachers — and to start off developing their reflection on teaching from observation and experience, rather than from 'received knowledge';
(2)   to encourage participants to value their own and each others' teaching and to learn from it;
(3)   to encourage participants to form support networks and create links with local professionals, and;
(4)   to encourage participants to reflect not just on their teaching but also on their own learning and how best to manage it.

Below, I review a number of ideas that may go some way to achieving these goals. The list contains ideas we actually tried out as well as others that have emerged with hindsight.

Tasks that require participants to record and analyse their own lessons

This was a feature of several tasks set as part of the RSA Dip. TFLA course. Participants had, for example, to analyse their use of questions or correction techniques. Such tasks effectively encouraged participants to look in detail at their own practice and to integrate any reading into their analysis of a concrete classroom interaction. These tasks tended to work better in the later stages of the course — some participants even took to recording their classes regularly — but initially, a few participants experienced them as quite alienating, as the following quote from a participant makes clear:

> The recording of lessons involved in some tasks, while sometimes illuminating and salutary, proved especially stressful for practical reasons, and sometimes changed the nature of the lesson, leading me

to think that I wasn't always learning from them what I should have been. . . . However, I do agree that it is very useful to be able to listen to the conduct of a lesson, and there seems little alternative to the process adopted here.

Tasks that require observations of colleagues or interviews with other teachers

As observers of others' teaching, participants can develop their own insight into what works and what doesn't, and thereby understand that 'theory' in teaching is in fact an attempt to generalise from practice, rather than something imposed from above. Such tasks could also serve to help isolated participants make contact with other teachers in their area.

Observation tasks from video/audio recordings as part of distance learning materials

To offset the stress associated with recording one's own class and the sometimes dissuasive 'inauthentic labour' that might be involved in negotiating access to other teachers' classes, audio and video recordings of language classes could play a role in providing a very powerful stimulus to thinking about teaching, particularly at a distance.

An effective local mentor scheme

This seems vital to help participants exploit their own teaching situation to the full. From our experience, it seems unrealistic to expect a mentor — normally a full-time teacher/supervisor — to do the job without any financial reward.

Assessed work that encourages a process, rather than a product, focus

One assignment that worked particularly well for distance learners on the RSA Dip. TFLA was the Personal Portfolio, defined in the Assessment Guide as 'an opportunity for you to present work in areas not covered by other assessed items . . . to illustrate your own development as a language teacher and the experiences that have contributed to your development'. A minimum of five written items was required. Participants were encouraged, for example, to keep learner diaries during the course and review their experiences as part of the Portfolio. Materials or teaching ideas developed and implemented during the course could also be written up and presented. The personal portfolio encouraged participants to reflect throughout the course on their own learning, on its ups and downs and on its breakthroughs.

Group work

Group projects, where several participants pool ideas and experience on a particular area of interest and write up a joint report, would seem an obvious way of encouraging distant participants to keep in touch and work with each other.

Resource and study groups

In Brighton, we asked participants to organise themselves at the first workshop into 'resource groups' of three, initially to facilitate the lending out of recommended books. In several cases, these 'resource groups' in fact became 'study support' groups. Their value was confirmed in participant reports such as this:

> Our local support group was extremely beneficial to us all throughout most of the course. Following a distance learning course can be very lonely. The problems involved in studying in this way and related to the course itself need to be shared. We would meet primarily to go through the units sent to us by post and to work through the tasks and discuss the books on the suggested reading list. The contributions we gave helped us all mutually to get more out of the course units and to understand more of what was expected of us as far as the assessed units were concerned. I normally left the meetings fired with enthusiasm and more able to tackle the tasks and assignments in a more focused way.

Ideas bulletins

To try and encourage participants to value and exchange their own teaching ideas and to maintain a sense of contact with each other and the local centre, an 'ideas bulletin' was launched. Participants sent in teaching ideas that had worked for them, which I then compiled, often adding ideas that had come up in written work and any I had picked up from observations or from colleagues. The ideas were presented anonymously and the bulletin photocopied and sent out to participants.

An Optimum Level of Support

I emerged from these two years' experience with a confirmed belief that there is in all learning an optimum level of support at which point learners are enabled to develop in confidence and as a result, learn on their own and from their own experience, integrating received knowledge as inspiration rather than as prescription. Too much support — and there will be a tendency to foster dependency and thereby deny learners an opportunity for finding their own path. Conversely, too little support and learners develop blocks and lose time stuck in confusion and as a result do not develop. How to dose the level of support is the biggest challenge in any teaching role — but it is all the more difficult in distance education, where the support and stimulation offered by peers is not readily available. Furthermore, there is not the regular interaction with learners that allows teachers to bring in line their teaching plans with perceived learner plans. Isolation is a problem for teachers in distance learning as well as for participants! But this merely confirms the importance of promoting and supporting autonomous learning on distance learning courses.

I have to say that the participants I worked with did emerge from the winter months of despondency when 'everything seemed to be going wrong'. I'd like to end with two quotes from participants' diaries (as they appeared in their Personal Portfolios) which illustrate a positive outcome, where the integration of received knowledge, experiential knowledge and reflection seems to have come about:

> I have learnt to anticipate learners' problems and difficulties and to consider their aims and purposes, been made aware of different approaches to teaching, found new interests, seen how necessary as well as beneficial it is to plan lessons or a series of lessons. Most importantly, I have learnt to assess and judge my teaching and the need to be critical and up-to-date with teaching principles and methods.

> The new me! . . . better setting of objectives, better planning of lessons, change of emphasis from teaching to learning, encouraging student autonomy. As far as my personal development as a teacher is concerned, I certainly have more confidence in what I am doing as a result of having a more systematic approach, underpinned by a better knowledge and understanding of the theoretical framework of current language teaching.

Note

1. This course, trialled on a national scale by IALS, Edinburgh between 1988 and 1990, was designed by Ian McGrath and written by Ian and other members of the IALS staff. It was withdrawn at the end of 1993, owing to lack of demand — a sad comment on employers' and funding bodies' awareness of the value of education and training.

References

Curran, C. (1976) *Counselling-Learning in Second Languages.* Apple River, IL: Apple River Press.

Higgins, J. (1988) *Language, Learners and Computers.* Harlow: Longman.

Rogers, A. (1986) *Teaching Adults.* Milton Keynes: Open University Press.

Wallace, M. (1991) *Training Foreign Language Teachers: A Reflective Approach.* Cambridge: Cambridge University Press.

Appendix 4.1

RSA DIPLOMA IN TEACHING FOREIGN LANGUAGES TO ADULTS

Language Centre, University of Brighton

OUTLINE COURSE PROGRAMME 1991-1992

SEPTEMBER: Preparatory Unit
Study Skills. Analysing Language. Lesson Planning.

OCTOBER: Workshop One
Communicative Language Teaching. The Adult Learner.
Classroom Organisation. The Psychology of Language Learning.

OCTOBER–JANUARY: Units One and Two
Theories of Language Learning and Teaching. Learner Strategies.
Error Analysis. Course Design and Syllabus Planning.
Teaching Listening Skills.

Tasks 1, 2, 3 and Assign. 1 to be submitted

JANUARY: Workshop Two
Learner Differences and Learner Autonomy. Specific Purposes
Teaching. Designing Communicative Tasks. Micro-teaching.

JANUARY–APRIL: Units Three and Four
Teaching Oral Skills. Correction and Explanation Techniques.
Teaching Grammar and Vocabulary. Reading and Writing Skills.

Tasks 4, 5, 6 to be submitted

APRIL: Workshop Three
Return to Lesson Planning. Using Authentic Materials.
Using Video. Micro-teaching.

APRIL–JULY: Unit Five
Learner Assessment. Differentiation.
Completion of outstanding coursework.

Task 7, Assign. 2, teaching manual and portfolio to be submitted

Appendix 4.2: Example of a Study Guide

UNITS FOUR (FROM WORKSHOP) AND FIVE (TO ARRIVE 6/4)
TASK 7, TEACHING MANUAL, ASSIGNMENT 2, PERSONAL
PORTFOLIO

1. MATERIALS DEVELOPMENT FOCUS

Materials for Vocabulary Development
- Read Unit 4 pp. 1–14.
- Read Gairns & Redman *Working with Words* photocopy.
- Reread MT's hand-outs from the workshop.

Differentiation
- Read Unit 5 on Differentiation and Appendix on Mixed Proficiency and work through unassessed tasks.
- If you're particularly interested in developing materials, look at David Nunan, *Designing Tasks for the Communicative Classroom,* or the books on reading skills by Christine Nuttall or Francoise Grellet.
- If you're more interested in materials for Special Purposes, look at course books such as *Working with French/German/Spanish* or get in touch with course tutors and tell us what kind of material you're interested in.

Implementation
- Try out some of these ideas with your classes.
- You can write about materials you have developed and how they worked with your class for your Personal Portfolio.
- You might comment on some of these ideas in your Teaching Manual.
- If you have chosen Task 7b, then design your materials, try them out with a class and write up task 7.

2. FINDING OUT ABOUT YOUR LEARNERS

- Read through Brief for Assignment 2B (Case Study).
- Re-read notes from Workshop and try to decide what exactly you want to investigate.
- Try to contact learner(s) whom you want to study.
- Glance back at Unit 1 Section on Individual Differences and The Good Language Learner.
- Do background reading photocopied: *Individual Differences* (McDonough).

- Then read photocopied Ellis article 'Classroom Learning Styles. . .'.
- If you're really interested in Learner Strategies, look at *Learner Strategies in Language Learning* particularly sections by J. Rubin, R. Vann & R. Abraham and A. Wenden.
- For light relief, inspiration and insight (useful for your Teaching Manual and Personal Portfolio), have a look at *Lingo*, BBC Publications.
- As a result of your reading, refine the focus of your study and decide how you are going to organise your research.
- Look at 'Case Study Tools' hand-out.
- Prepare tests, questionnaires, list of interview questions etc.
- Do your investigation and write up your Assignment 2B.

5 Pre-service Training for Language Teachers: Face-to-Face or at a Distance?

IAN MCGRATH

Introduction

In essence, this paper is a response. It is a response, first, to the proliferation over the last few years of distance-training programmes aimed at those with little or no experience of language teaching, a development on which I have commented on a previous occasion (McGrath, 1992). More positively, it is a response to the suggestion in a recent research paper (Davis, 1990) that we should question the assumption that underlies most UK-based initial TEFL training: that the intensive face-to-face mode of training is necessarily the most effective.

Pragmatism and Education: A Historical Perspective

Between the two extremes of distance only and face-to-face only lies what I shall call 'the mixed-mode programme', which combines distance and face-to-face components. UK-based programmes of this kind have existed for some time, of course. Lowe (1983, 1988) discusses some of the design features of the Cambridge/RSA Dip. TEFLA[1] distance training programme established by International House at the beginning of the 1980s; Winn-Smith (1984) describes the Eaton Hall distance training programmes[2] which ran during the 1980s; and Parker (1991) offers a brief description of the programmes run by Sheffield Hallam University[3] (see also Haworth and Parker, and Parker and Graham, Chapters 6 and 12). However, what seems to have prompted the development of distance components in these programmes was a pragmatic or logistical motive: if trainees were unable to come to the UK for a full-length face-to-face course or follow one locally, the thinking went, an alternative was to take at least part of the course to them. In Winn-Smith's summary of the factors that led to this 'externalisation of training' (op.cit.: 20) at Eaton Hall, the key elements are 'demand' and cost, while Lowe states unequivocally: 'we had to replicate, as far as possible, the circumstances of a face-to-face course' (1983: 38).

These may have been the initial motivations, but institutions were not slow to recognise the educational benefits specific to distance education. Having summarised the factors that prompted the setting up of the Eaton Hall programmes, Winn-Smith goes on to list a number of additional advantages of distance education — advantages that, he confesses, only became apparent at a later stage. These include: extending course content at minimal cost to trainees; catering, through specially developed modules, for context-specific needs; and post-course up-dating. Writing about the programmes at Sheffield Hallam University, Parker also refers to a shift in awareness concerning the potential of distance education:

> . . . what may originally have started as a system designed to provide teacher education economically in an environment where resources were traditionally limited has grown both in its original scope *and in its original aims.*

The aims of our distance learning systems can now be summarised as:

- overall cost reduction
- encouragement towards process orientation
- de-intensification of residential blocks
- improving the mode of delivery
- improving participant morale.

(Parker, 1991: 17; emphasis added)

The remainder of Parker's short article is an elaboration of these five aims.

Although I recognise that pragmatic considerations are important, my main purpose in this paper is to extend what I think of as the educational argument for distance training for language teachers. I shall be presenting, first, a rationale for distance programmes as one form of continuing professional education; and will then go on to argue that for the target group I have in mind, pre-service trainees in the UK, the mixed-mode programme is the most appropriate.

Levels of Training

Perraton (1993) makes a distinction between three categories of training provision, here presented in Table 5.1:

Table 5.1 Categories of training provision

Pre-service	
	Initial training
In-service	
Continuing education	

It would be tempting to comment on the implied distinction between 'training' and 'education' (Perraton's terms), but for the purposes of the present paper I wish merely to draw attention to the value of Perraton's broad distinction between those who have already successfully completed a period of qualifying training and those who have not; and within the latter group, between those with teaching experience and those without. Many of my own generation (who graduated from university in the mid-late 1960s) were only aware of the existence of one TEFL qualification[4], the one-year Postgraduate Certificate of Education (TEFL) offered by a number of universities. One of the entry requirements for such programmes was that applicants had to have a minimum of two years' relevant teaching experience; those who were accepted for this, their first (or initial) period of training, were thus, in experiential terms if not in terms of actual working conditions, practising teachers following an in-service course. Now that many more qualifications and programmes are available, I would guess that the majority of would-be TEFL teachers in the UK seek training before teaching. It is the needs of this group, pre-service trainees in the UK, that is my principal concern in this chapter.

It may seem a little perverse, therefore, if I first discuss the relevance of particular programme delivery modes in relation to *continuing* education. The logic of this will, I hope, become clear.

Programme Formats for Continuing Education

There are strong arguments for considering distance learning as a mode of delivery for the continuing education of teachers (or any practising professionals, in fact).

Cost

(1) no travel or subsistence costs;
(2) no loss of income (except for those who have to give up private lessons);
(3) no teacher replacement costs (e.g. no financial costs; no diminution in teacher quality caused by substitution).

Convenience

(1) to individual (no domestic disruption, other than that caused by home-study);
(2) to institution (no need for substitute);
(3) to pupils (continuity).

Flexibility

(1) self-pacing (scope for this varies from scheme to scheme);
(2) study options (selection, sequence)[5].

Access

(1) greater number able to benefit;
(2) wider range of possible participants.

Relevance

(1) teaching context can be exploited as data source and testing-ground for new ideas;
(2) reflection on theory and practice encouraged by context of study (learning while teaching) and by spaced input.

In relation to continuing professional education, the last point — relevance — seems to me particularly important. One way of building in such relevance is through tasks that encourage teachers to look analytically at their own teaching context, including their learners, and their own teaching (e.g. using recordings or learner questionnaires). Such tasks can serve a variety of purposes. For instance, they can stimulate the kind of systematic self-evaluation that enables individuals to set their own agenda for change; they can encourage the search for alternatives, through reading and perhaps discussion with colleagues; and they can provide an opportunity not only for the integration of theory and practice but also for the development of theory out of practice. My own experience of running distance-training programmes for practising language teachers suggests that they are perceived as practical because relevant to practice (cf. Lowe, 1983, who equates practicality with the face-to-face component). There are a number of well-attested disadvantages in distance learning (e.g. psychological isolation, stress, difficulty in obtaining resource materials). Nevertheless, my general conclusion, based on five years' experience of language-teacher education at a distance is that provided a programme exploits participants' own daily experience and working environment in such a way that they are encouraged not only to make connections between theory and practice but also to generate through reflection their own theories, it is more likely to be successful in promoting steady long-term change than a programme with comparable content which is delivered face-to-face. I have two main reasons for thinking this:

(1) in face-to-face programmes of any length, participants are normally cut off from their classrooms (the obvious exceptions to this would be part-time in-service programmes in the UK and overseas);
(2) the uninterrupted diet of instruction, even in the form of tasks or workshops, frequently results in mental indigestion.

One result of these two circumstances is that participants on intensive programmes frequently complain that after a certain stage they are incapable of processing anything new, and I would guess that for this reason, as well as the natural process of forgetting — sometimes exacerbated by a long gap between the completion of the programme and the resumption of teaching much of what is taught in an intensive programme evaporates before it can be applied in the classroom.

I have suggested that distance-training programmes can not only make a contribution to continuing education for teachers but may even be superior in some respects to face-to-face programmes. Let us now turn to the possible role of distance programmes in pre-service training.

The Objectives of Pre-service Training

There are at least two major differences between those undergoing pre-service training and those following in-service training (be it initial or continuing). Pre-service trainees lack a basis of *knowledge*, and they lack a basis of *experience*. This is not to say that when they start their training they are *tabula rasa*, any more than language learners are: they have relevant knowledge (of the language they will be teaching, for instance) and relevant experience (of learning, of language learning, of teachers, of teaching institutions), and one of the questions we should be asking ourselves as teacher educators is how to make use of this prior learning. In fact, the question that we tend to ask when designing pre-service programmes is more directed towards terminal behaviour: how to ensure that trainees have the necessary knowledge and skill to function effectively in classrooms and, by implication, what this knowledge and skill consists of. In other words, our concern is more with putting things in than getting things out.

Actually, the question about prior learning and the question about future needs are equally relevant, and they are related. If we can specify both target knowledge and skill *and* prior learning, we are also in a position to specify the content and goals of the programme. As a needs-analysis procedure, this is just as true for in-service training. The main difference between pre-service and, at the other extreme, continuing education, is that whereas in continuing education the emphasis will be on the further development of the existing knowledge-base and skills (pedagogic and/or linguistic), the primary goal of pre-service training is to establish such a knowledge-base. In the case of those teaching their native language, since a relatively high degree of competence in the use of the language has to be assumed, this knowledge-base will include knowledge about the language and about how to teach it, which in turn includes some understanding of language learners and their needs. Theoretical knowledge in itself is not enough, of course; trainees must also be able to apply that knowledge in planning and executing lessons — in other words, be able to integrate and operationalise the various knowledge elements in a (relatively) skilled manner.

Acquiring Knowledge and Skills

This brings us to the issue of how knowledge and skills are acquired. It is generally recognised that teaching skills are developed through practice and that, although observation of other teachers may play a contributory role, the essential components of that practice in an initial stage of training are regular contact with students and feedback from an experienced observer on one's teaching performance. (On the various functions of observation, see Maingay, 1988.) The relationship between knowledge (here representing both the result of initial instruction and learning from observer feedback) and skill can be represented in Figure 5.1.

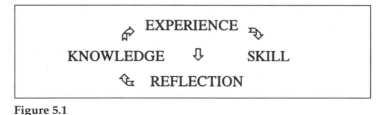

Figure 5.1

Knowledge, according to this model, can only become skill through suitable experience; and experience distilled through personal reflection serves to refine and extend the knowledge-base. (The literature abounds with other, more complex models. See e.g. Kolb, 1984; Boud, Keogh & Walker, 1985; Wallace, 1991.)

At the heart of skill-acquisition, I have suggested, lies experience, and reflection on that experience. What of knowledge ? Certain kinds of relevant knowledge also derive from classroom experiences (for instance, knowledge about the likely result of particular actions or about the nature of learner difficulties), but there is a body of objective or descriptive knowledge that is more appropriately learned by other means. I am thinking here of analytical knowledge about the target language (and the learners' language if the teaching context is monolingual) and knowledge about the principles on which teaching can be planned and conducted; I am also thinking of awareness-raising in relation to cultural differences, individual learner differences, and teaching aids and resources. True, observation of experienced teachers may be a valuable element in the acquisition of these kinds of knowledge, but it is no substitute for sustained and systematic study, especially as far as the language system is concerned.

Programme Formats for Pre-service Training

The difficulty for the designer of a pre-service course is to find a satisfactory compromise between these two requirements: to provide for the acquisition of a solid knowledge-base (knowledge about the language, about teaching, about learners); and to provide the experience without which there is no opportunity for the acquisition of practical teaching skills. (This tension might be less acute in overseas situations where pre-service trainees are following a two- or three-year programme; but there is the added problem that attention also has to be given to trainees' skills as users of the target language (McGrath, 1974)).

Four-week face-to-face programmes

In the UK context, where trainees' time and particularly money are the main issue, the typical pre-service programme leading to internationally recognised qualifications such as the Cambridge/RSA Cert. TEFLA (CTEFLA) or the Trinity College Certificate in TESOL is an intensive face-to-face programme that lasts for four weeks. Whatever the strengths of such programmes — and they have undoubted strengths — they also have two major disadvantages: from the point of view of the trainee they are relatively expensive[6] and if one takes training needs into account they are too short.

Dellar (1990) examines the performance in a Moroccan context of three 'novice teachers' who have completed initial training programmes and concludes that 'the UK based training . . . seemed to have failed to equip them for a considerable range of pedagogic functions' (70), especially for teaching in an overseas monolingual context. She categorises these functions under the following headings:

- problems of control — insufficient training for certain aspects of teaching or types of class;
- inappropriate methodology (lack of theoretical understanding);
- lesson planning difficulties.

Davis's (1990) study of the four-week courses leading to the CTEFLA identifies a rather different set of weaknesses in newly certificated teachers working in UK language schools. Such teachers, according to Davis's ten informants ('pedagogic supervisors'), manifest an inability to:

- analyse and teach grammatical structures;
- understand and teach pronunciation effectively;
- diagnose and cope with students' language problems.

The differences between the lists offered by Dellar and Davis are not surprising, given the fact that in Davis's case, multilingual adult classes provide both the context for training and for subsequent teaching. More significantly, their conclusions are similar. Davis suggests that the weaknesses of CTEFLA-trained teachers are due to the tendency in such short programmes (100 plus hours) to concentrate 'on practical classroom techniques to the almost complete exclusion of the theoretical basis for these practices' (Davis, 1990: 8). He argues that 'a practitioner needs to be at least aware of the more theoretical levels (approach and design) to operate effectively the procedural aspects of a methodology' (Davis, 1990: 12). Parker (1991: 17) makes the further point that if the trainees see the course as complete in itself and themselves as 'final products' this may inhibit their future professional development.

Distance-training programmes

The obvious alternative to a relatively expensive, relatively short CTEFLA course is a distance-training programme, and the distance-training programmes advertised each week in the *Guardian* and the *Times Educational Supplement* appear to be, comparatively, both reasonably priced and flexible as far as length of study is concerned. Judging from their publicity material, some course-providers also operate an open-access policy with regard to educational qualifications and first language, and this latter consideration may make their programmes particularly attractive to non-native speakers of English hoping to gain a qualification that will enable them to work in other countries. Most important for the argument presented here, however, is the fact that many of these programmes are delivered only through distance-learning materials and do not contain a compulsory teaching-practice component.

This leads me to suggest that, despite their convenience, distance-only programmes are severely limited as far as the needs of pre-service trainees are concerned because *they fail to provide the structured classroom experience through which teaching skills are developed.* For those trainees who are not already expert users of the target language, the absence of face-to-face instruction in the language may also be a severe disadvantage. The question of whether the qualification that lies at the end of the programme has a market value is a separate issue, but one that is not unrelated.

Where does this leave us? If the findings of Dellar and Davis are generalisable — and the smallness of their samples must leave this open to some doubt — then the four-week face-to-face programmes may not provide a satisfactory theoretical grounding. The distance-only programmes, on the other hand, lack the crucial dimension of classroom practice. The solution, wherever possible, would seem to be to combine the two in a mixed-mode programme.

A mixed-mode pre-service programme

For pre-service trainees, a mixed-mode programme, as we have seen from the preceding discussion, has certain advantages over a single-mode programme, be it face-to-face only or distance-only, in particular the fact that trainees are likely to emerge with a better balance of basic knowledge and skills.

This should not be taken to mean that a mixed-mode programme of initial training can be complete in itself. As Parker (1991) notes, one advantage of a mixed-mode programme is that it not only prolongs the educational experience but also helps trainees to get the intensive, i.e. residential, part of that experience into proportion, and to see the programme as a whole as part of a continuing process of self-development.

Research Questions

Where institutions do opt for a mixed-mode programme, this raises a number of theoretical and practical issues, three of which seem to me to be of particular interest:

(1) What is the basic minimum content for a pre-service programme for no specified context ? (This question should be asked, of course, by any programme provider.)

(2) What criteria should determine the distribution of content across delivery modes (i.e. distance vs face-to-face) ?

(3) What principles should determine the sequencing (of delivery modes, not of content) ?

Before we can tackle the first issue, we need more information, of the sort provided by Davis and Dellar on the shortcomings of novice teachers, and by Laskaridou (1990), who used job analysis techniques to look at the functions carried out by practising EFL teachers. In other words, we need to base the objectives of pre-service programmes on a thoroughgoing analysis of the core need of the trainees. We also need to consider how to cater for context-specific needs: teaching young children or monolingual classes and teaching English for specific purposes.

The second question, which delivery mode can best facilitate learning, is one that naturally exercises designers of distance-learning programmes, but what is normally at issue is the choice of medium (e.g. print, audio, print plus audio, video, telephone, computer). In the case of mixed-mode programmes, the range of options is greatly extended in that, within the context of a face-to-face component, we can more easily exploit the possibility for group learning (through, e.g., paired observation, microteaching, peer-teaching, and discussion based on individual or group tasks) as well as for tutor demonstration and tutor feedback on trainees' performance skills. However, since time is short and the expectations of participants high we obviously need to give careful thought not only to the general question of whether a topic is best treated during the face-to-face component or during a distance learning component, but also to the relationship during a face-to-face block between intensity and intake, to variety of activity and pace, and to the affective as well as the cognitive dimension. One of the most crucial contributions of a face-to-face component may be its power to provide reassurance and support for the individual.

In relation to the third issue, the sequencing of face-to-face and distance components, Davis (1990) proposes a three-phase programme: distance learning — intensive block — induction period in an EFL school. The Sheffield Hallam pattern for their pre-service programme comprises a sandwich of 12 weeks distance — 4 weeks intensive — 3 weeks distance, a total of 19 weeks (Parker 1991); Eaton Hall's shorter sandwich was 8–4–2 (Winn-Smith, 1984). Although my own instinct would also be for the sandwich, I think I would opt for a more balanced distribution of time over the distance-learning blocks on the grounds that the sooner participants meet tutors and each other the better. In the first phase, in addition to providing language awareness materials of the sort envisaged by Davis, I would ideally want to prime trainees for the face-to-face element by incorporating an observation element (video and live observation); and since I am far from sure that Davis's third phase is practicable, my third-phase materials would consist of teacher support packs and tasks (including observation) to encourage reflection.

I have deliberately sounded a hypothetical note in these last remarks. One reason for this is that I am not currently involved in pre-service training, and another is that we need a good deal more research before we are in a position to judge between the various options available. One strand in this research ought to be trainee-centred and longitudinal: we need to know how trainees feel about the effectiveness of particular procedures and their appropriateness for particular purposes, and how their own perceptions of their needs change over time.

We can be certain about one thing, though: that trainees who have just completed a period of pre-service training are merely 'EFL-initiated' (British Council, 1988, cited in Davis, 1990: 18) and will continue to need structured guidance. Whether this induction into 'real' teaching should actually form an integral part of the training, as proposed by Davis or be an extension of it, best done in the context of the first post, as in Dellar (1990), is yet another question that merits discussion by all those concerned — validating bodies, trainers, employers and trainees.

Notes

1. Cambridge/Royal Society of Arts Diploma in the Teaching of English as a Foreign Language to Adults.
2. Eaton Hall closed in 1992.
3. Formerly Sheffield City Polytechnic.
4. A four-week course was set up at International House in 1962 (Haycraft 1988, in Duff, T. (ed.) 1988). The one-year PGCE courses were eligible for LEA grants and offered the further benefit, in due course, of 'qualified teacher status' and access to posts in the British state sector.
5. See also the paper in this volume by Cowan.
6. At the time of writing, some programmes leading to the CTEFLA cost in excess of £800.

References

Boud, D., Keogh, R. and Walker, D. (eds) (1985) *Reflection: Turning Experience into Learning.* London: Kogan Page.

Davis, H. (1990) *The Four-week CTEFLA Course: A First Step Towards Evaluation.* Cambridge: University of Cambridge Local Examinations Syndicate.

Dellar, G. (1990) The needs of 'novice' teachers: a case study. In Roberts, J. (ed.) (1990): 62–77.

Duff, T. (ed.) (1988) *Explorations in Teacher Training: Problems and Issues.* London: Longman.

Haycraft, J. (1988) The first International House preparatory course: an historical overview. In Duff, T. (ed.) (1988): 1–9.

Kolb, D. (1984) *Experiential Learning.* Englewood Cliffs, NJ: Prentice Hall.

Laskaridou, D. (1990) Job analysis and the design of pre-service teacher training courses. In Roberts, J. (ed.) (1990): 7–34.

Lowe, T. (1983) Coming face to face with distance teacher training. *Modern English Teacher* 11 (1): 38–40.

Lowe, T. (1988) A 'correspondence course' for teachers of English: a case history. In Duff, T. (ed.) (1988): 50–63.

Maingay, P. (1988) Observation for training, development or assessment? In Duff, T. (ed.) (1988): 118–131.

McGrath, I. (1974) Language skills for language teachers. *English Language Teaching Journal* 28(4), 296–299.

McGrath, I. (1992) Teacher education through distance learning: A matter of faith? Paper presented at IATEFL/ALL Conference, Edinburgh, April 1992.

Parker, R. (1991) Distance learning as a component of TESOL courses. In *Distance Learning.* English Studies Issue No. 7. London: The British Council: 16–18.

Perraton, H. (ed.) (1993) *Distance Education for Teacher Training.* London: Routledge.

Roberts, J. (ed.) (1990) *Initial Training and the First Year in School.* CALS Workpapers Vol.1. Centre for Applied Language Studies, University of Reading.

Wallace, M. (1991) *Training Foreign Language Teachers: A Reflective Approach.* Cambridge: Cambridge University Press.

Winn-Smith, B. (1984) Distance learning in teacher training. *World Language English* 4(1), 20–27.

6 The Contribution of a Face-to-Face Component in Initial Teacher Training[1] at a Distance

TERESA HAWORTH AND RAY PARKER

Insight which dawns slowly seems to me to have more lasting effect than fitful idealism which is unlikely to hold out for long (Carl Gustav Jung).

Introduction

This paper sets out not to justify the distance-learning component of initial teacher education courses nor to account for it in terms of its being a substitute for more conventional modes of teacher-education. Instead it builds on the premise that distance learning can probably deliver parts of a teacher-education course better than other modes and that when linked appropriately to a suitably designed direct-contact component a synthesis of approach is achieved that enriches the overall teacher education experience.

What is the Function of Initial Teacher Education in TESOL?

It is one of the functions of teacher educators to prepare teachers for a future that *we* have predicted for them. We base that prediction on our combined experiential knowledge of the field of TESOL, the additional predictive knowledge built into the guidance documents and syllabuses of examination boards, our contemporary experiences and observations, etc.

On the face of it this might seem to be a reasonable overall aim for initial TESOL teacher education. Long ago, however, we realised that this was nowhere near enough. Now we try even harder to prepare our teachers for all those futures that we have *not* predicted and that are, indeed, unpredictable. Common sense tells us that these futures will be far more numerous and varied than the particular scenarios that we may have envisaged and our general response to this need has been confirmed and encouraged in recent years by the published views of Richards & Nunan (1990), Widdowson (1990) and Wallace (1991) among others.

This conviction, then, translates itself into a number of requirements that we make of courses and, by extension, course members.

The Requirements of Initial TESOL Teacher Education Courses

The requirements are that the course should provide and course members progressively acquire:

(1) a knowledge base:
    1.1 of the subject;
    1.2 of general current pedagogy related to the teaching of that subject;
(2) relevant technical classroom skills (e.g. using a tape-recorder, organising pair and group work, etc.);
(3) procedural skills (i.e. linking the selection from the acquired repertoire of 2 to an understanding of 1.2 informed by an understanding of 1.1);
(4) a reflective orientation to 1, 2 and 3.

There are, we believe, at least three pre-requisites for the development and exercise of 4.

A desire to reflect

This is at least partly a conscious, directed process which may at times be quite uncomfortable. There may well need to be a conscious act of will involved to overcome and work through the discomfort experienced. Wallace (1991: 166) points out the difficulty: 'The role. . . of the language teacher as reflective practitioner, is a very demanding one. There are many understandable reasons why such a role might be avoided or declined.'

The means to reflect

There needs to be information available to enrich and even inform the process of reflection. Reflection is thus not seen as contemplation or meditation, which might take place entirely internally. At the very least this implies access to reference materials for example. More than anything, however, this means that the Educating Institution has the duty to ensure that teachers, when reflecting, are asking themselves the right questions. Teachers must be 'weaned off' their understandable preoccupation with classroom techniques. Richards and Nunan (1990: 201) put it well: 'The critically reflective teacher is one who moves beyond the search for instructional techniques alone (asking "how to" questions) to a concern for "what" and "why" questions' (see also Bartlett 1990).

Time to reflect

Reflection is not seen as an instant inspirational activity. It is not a linguistic accident that the word 'reflection' routinely collocates with the word 'mature'.

Can These Requirements Be Met Through Distance Learning?

The answer to this question obviously depends on the particular requirement being considered.

In the case of 1.1, the knowledge base of the subject, the answer seems to be 'yes' — almost completely. A glance at the syllabuses currently in use at the TESOL Centre for the Language Awareness and Phonology Units of Distance Learning should reassure most experienced practitioners in this field that there is little or nothing here that cannot be dealt with through the traditional media of distance learning — books, other printed materials, cassettes, etc. (See Appendix 6.1.)

To a lesser extent 1.2 (relevant pedagogical concerns) and 3 can be started in distance learning mode. Again a syllabus might save a lot of words here (see Appendix 6.2).

Requirement 2 cannot be met outside a direct contact phase.

Requirement 4 is contained within the distance learning process itself and Figure 6.1 will help to illustrate this.

Can These Requirements Be Better Met Through Distance Learning?

We have become convinced over the years that the answer to this question in the cases of requirements 1.1 and 4 is certainly 'yes'. The reasons for this are fairly self-evident but perhaps need a little justification. There is some pressure on teacher educators to practise what they preach and

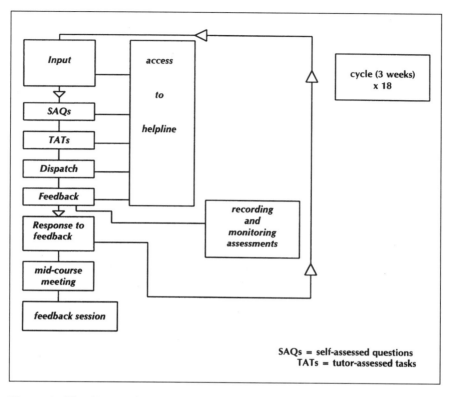

Figure 6.1 The distance learning process

nowhere is this more true than in language teaching where we have seen a tendency in the last decade or two to take seriously the precepts of various methodologies collectively described as humanistic and to focus our general teaching attitudes towards learner-centredness[2].

Many of the topics in the syllabuses in Appendices 6.1 and 6.2 could easily be dealt with during a face-to-face course through brainstorming, groupwork, demonstration, etc. This would, however, rob our course members of precious private opportunities to securely rehearse new insights and would further deny them the substantial time required for doing so.

Education or Training?

It is this same concern to avoid terminology that is obsolete, in the sense of being inappropriate and inadequate to describe the processes involved, which leads to our commitment to the term 'teacher *education*', even in the context of initial courses. Here too, the lexical preference is significant: it expresses the conviction that initial training courses, of their nature, provide only a partial and oversimplified response to a very complex set of challenges.

Initial education courses, on the other hand, overtly set out to provide a total learning experience that responds to the future needs of the teacher as both practitioner and innovator. In other words, education courses, in line with a legitimate *product* orientation, must, as has already been argued, give participants a relevant knowledge base, equip them with a 'repertoire' of proven techniques and procedures and provide them with a range of reliable responses to predictable problems. Equally important, however, is their concern to 'trigger' other much more complex *processes* that, in developing such attributes as awareness, autonomy and flexibility, take participants beyond the 'how' and even the 'what' of teaching, to consider the 'whether' and the 'why'.

From Distance-Learning to Direct Contact: A Global Perspective

The overall commitment to what is currently referred to as a 'reflective practitioner' model of teacher education and, within this, our view of the function of the distance-learning phase, has an inevitable impact on the tone and texture of the direct-contact phase. This means an approach whose 'tone' is appropriately non-directive and whose 'texture' is of suitably 'loose weave' to allow for innovative changes to the pattern. Given the very wide age-range and broad spectrum of experience typical of participant groups, such an approach satisfies the need for individual variation, while never losing sight of an indispensable degree of overall coherence and cohesion.

Put another way, a good initial teacher education course has to be like the one-size T-shirt: it has to 'fit' people of vastly different shapes and sizes, while allowing all of them to feel and look good according to their own individual attributes.

Dawning Insights

At an earlier stage in our experience, the approach to course delivery tended to be partly conditioned by a perception of the distance-learning phase as something of a 'faute de mieux' and of the distance-learner as someone whose lonely suffering had somehow to be compensated for by the sheer amount of classroom contact, with theory and practice being dispensed from 'jug' to 'mug', via a fairly narrow range of delivery-modes.

As the inherent and distinctive attributes of distance-learning have become clear, this value-for-money, quantity-driven model of course structure and style of delivery has given way, incrementally, to a much more quality-oriented approach, more in keeping with our conception of the direct-contact phase as providing experiences that essentially complement and extend that which has gone before. The result is a 'leaner and fitter' course programme, realised in a flexible environment that, by allowing maximum scope for participation and interaction, seeks to nurture the propensity to reflection and autonomy that the distance-learning phase seeks actively to stimulate.

What's in a Name?

This basic course motivation is reflected in many ways, not least in the importance that is again attached to calling things by appropriate names. In a contemporary academic climate where the use of discipline specific terminology can all too easily degenerate into purposeless jargon, it is worth stressing that this care in choosing terms is not exercised in pursuit of political correctness. Rather it acknowledges the undeniable power of words to shape perceptions and to exert a benign or malignant influence on attitudes.

In this way, the linguistic 'climate' of the direct-contact phase actively provides a language awareness dimension and thus becomes part and parcel of the whole educational experience. The preferred terms are an explicit acknowledgement of the benefits believed to accrue from the distance-learning phase and hence of the tremendous potential waiting to be imaginatively exploited. As such, their connotations are an important reminder to us of our responsibilities and obligations as tutors. Inasmuch as they occur naturally and spontaneously in the input data, they also give an implicit signal to course participants *vis-à-vis* their future learners.

A number of these terminological choices, and their translation into programme content, are addressed in detail in the review of course components that follows. For immediate illustrative purposes, though, it is perhaps worthwhile considering the preference for the term 'course member' or 'participant' as compared with the more commonly used term 'trainee'.

The former terms explicitly recognise that such participants bring with them, not only the varying outcomes of the common distance-learning experience, but also their contributions as individuals from a broad range of educational and professional backgrounds. By expressing and demonstrating respect for what the individual has to offer, tutors can generate increased confidence. This encourages more active participation, which in turn enriches the group encounter. This experience of being valued as an individual and as a group member seems bound to shape positively the attitude of participants *vis-à-vis* their own learners.

From Words to Deeds

In the rest of this chapter we focus on a number of aspects that illustrate particularly well the participative, interactional and reflective dimensions of the course experience and therefore the mutually reinforcing interplay between the distance-learning and direct-contact phases. The selected aspects relate to programme delivery, in-course teaching and in-course assessment.

Programme Delivery — Sharing Responsibility

Input sessions

Teachers are frequently exhorted to become facilitators of learning. Teacher educators must therefore practise what they preach and demonstrate that in a learning encounter no one has a monopoly of the prerogative to initiate input. This means that the definitive 'shape' of these sessions cannot be determined in advance. Nor can they be allowed to be totally amorphous. They simply have to be conceived and realised with sufficient flexibility to accommodate the varying needs, wants, expectations and pre-course experience of all participants. Within these same constraints, there has to be maximum opportunity for involvement, on whatever basis the individual course member feels 'comfortable' with. In providing such opportunities, tutors are practising rather than simply preaching the virtue of facilitation.

With some groups, for example those with a strong 'model preference' in favour of a 'knowing' tutor, this very flexibility of approach can result in a predominantly tutor-led mode of interaction. However, even here, tutors would attempt to avoid domination via the appropriate use of referential, as opposed to display, questions and by encouraging a variety of interaction patterns.

With others, more varied patterns of interaction often occur quite spontaneously. Neither reaction should be considered intrinsically more valid or valuable, since each responds to different situations of group needs. Over the duration of a typical course, the preferred interactional mode tends quite naturally to vary depending on such factors as participants' familiarity with, understanding of and motivation for the topic under consideration, generally resulting in a fairly balanced 'diet' overall.

In all contexts, there has to be space for mutually acceptable negotiation. The individual, whether course member or tutor, must respect the needs of the group and the group must accommodate the needs of the individual.

Self-managed time: Extending the practice of autonomy

It has recently become standard practice to offer a significant amount of negotiable self-managed time as an integral part of the overall course programme. The motivation behind this innovative programme element is more or less self-explanatory and its existence certainly self-justifying. Learning of any kind needs time and space. But, this should not mean merely the 'crumbs' and 'corners' of time left free by the average 'money's worth' time-table, but what has now come to be referred to, very appositely, as 'quality' time.

Formal endorsement of this notion within the course programme gives it the status necessary to be taken seriously during the course. Just as importantly, it encourages course members to appreciate that the regular deployment of such 'quality' time, the value of which they have already become aware of during the distance-learning phase, will remain an essential ingredient of their on-going development as effective teachers. If participants are to take on the role, as Widdowson (1990) argues they should, of 'mediators' between theory and practice, then they need time to work themselves into this role, time to make the principled decisions that prevent teaching being a mere reflection of current fads and fashions.

By definition, the 'ownership' of this time is exclusively the domain of course participants. The objective in making such time available is to nurture the propensity to autonomy that one hopes has been stimulated during the distance-learning phase. Hence, any attempts at externally defining 'good' ways of deploying it are unacceptable, contradictory and probably counter-productive. External agents have the prerogative to 'invade' this space only if invited to. Productive and creative use of this time is generally reflected in the quality of the individual member's input to the course. This in turn determines the quality of outcome for that individual and for the group and hence the course's long-term contribution to the professional development of participants.

Best-lesson workshops

Participant-led sessions are an important aspect of an approach to course delivery that recognises the value of a multi-directional flow of information. They also provide an important scenario for pooling the insights gained by individuals from the in-course teaching experience. As such they encourage a collaborative spirit and are instrumental in developing and refining skills of self-evaluation.

Again, ownership of these sessions lies with course members, so there are no set norms or standard requirements. Fairly typically, however, a workshop consists of three or four individual course members sharing with their peers and a participating tutor, in whatever format they prefer and according to criteria determined by them, their personal 'best' in-course teaching experience. This will naturally have involved them in reviewing their teaching journal (see below) and in the best of circumstances will generate a productive amount of group interaction.

As such, this particular programme element can be seen to encapsulate a wide range of important features: it is highly process-oriented; it is naturally reflective; it encourages participation and collaboration; and its ultimate value is a function of the interaction which it generates.

In-course Teaching — Varied Interactional Patterns

Teaching-liaison meetings

Within an initial teacher education course, participants need a reliable support network, and indeed have the right to expect that this will be an integral part of the overall course programme. Since they must also come to appreciate the value of productive collaboration with colleagues, it is vital that participants do not see tutors as the sole providers of support and guidance. In other words, a system of peer-support must operate to complement that provided by tutors.

These teaching-liaison meetings serve precisely this function, by making available a forum for pre- and post-lesson consultation with other course members. On the purely practical level, these meetings help to ensure that everyone is up-to-date regarding what the various learner groups have covered so far. In that they make it possible for teachers to exchange information and reactions related to a whole range of live classroom experiences and issues, they become an invaluable source of in-course professional development.

The teaching journal

Central to the future personal and professional development of course participants is their ability, quite literally, to stand on their own two feet. This means that participants on initial education courses must come to realise that they themselves are the most vital component of their support network. Their future ability to make sense of experience and hence to grow and develop as teachers crucially depends on qualities such as self-reliance and skills such as self-evaluation. Hence the need for participants to engage in 'critical monologue', for example, via the keeping of a teaching journal.

A journal well kept performs a multitude of benign functions, particularly if a pre-lesson reflection stage is advised. This generally results in a more rigorous thinking through of the various lesson phases and hopefully therefore greater awareness of implications and more accurate anticipation of difficulties. Participants thus achieve a better quality in terms of process (of planning) and product (the lesson), thereby ensuring an enhanced experience for teacher and learners alike.

Post-lesson debriefings

This item is intimately linked to the previous one, both being integral to the model of delayed interactive feedback which underpins the total approach to in-course teaching. This approach overtly rejects the notion of teaching as performance, being essentially process and development orientated.

In procedural terms, the sequence is as follows:

(1) The lesson is planned and prepared — inputs here include:
    (a) general course input;
    (b) specific teaching component guidelines;
    (c) textbook and teachers' book;
    (d) teaching liaison meetings — i.e. peer support;
    (e) tutorial guidance and reassurance.
(2) The pre-lesson reflection stage of the journal is completed.
(3) A 'during-observation' observer-focusing sheet may be prepared by the teacher partly as a result of 1 and 2 above and partly through reflection on previous teaching events.
(4) The lesson takes place with an observing tutor present.

(5) After the lesson, teacher and observing tutor agree a mutually convenient time for the debriefing — usually the next day at the latest.

(6) *Before* debriefing, the teacher completes appropriate journal entries and the observing tutor writes-up the lesson 'report'.

(7) The debriefing meeting takes place.

(8) Both the lesson and the quality of the debriefing session are assessed but not graded.

(9) At the end of the course the assessment of this event contributes to the grading of the participant's teaching.

The quality of the debriefing meeting is dependent in the first instance not only on the fact of the delay, but just as importantly on the use to which both teacher and tutor put this delay: in other words, it is a reflective opportunity for both parties. This seems essential if both are to achieve a balanced overview, taking due account of product related considerations, but placing them in an overall process perspective.

The quality of the outcome depends also on the nature of the interaction. Both parties have equal prerogative to take the role of initiator or responder and equal responsibility to ensure a two-way flow of exchanges. This is not to deny the tutor's right, indeed duty, to focus on those aspects of 'performance' that in their professional opinion need modifying in some way, but it also recognises the corresponding right of the teacher to measure these opinions against their own and their duty to adopt a proactive stance with regard to their own teaching.

Shortly before the end of the course all observing tutors meet and one overall assessment grade is given for the in-course teaching. Final grades are agreed only when tutors have compared and discussed their lesson and debriefing 'reports' on individual course members. The final grade, while inevitably summative, is thus the product of a highly reflective process.

In-course Assessment — Holistic and Reflective

Open-book reviews of learning

Over time the previous use of in-course tests administered under examination conditions came to appear non-congruent with the generally reflective and interactive character of the course as a whole. A relatively recent innovation has therefore been to introduce open-book reviews that involve course members in actively reprocessing the distance-learning modules in order to respond to a range of questions — questions not in themselves radically different from those used in earlier procedures.

In this way, a positive outcome is less reliant on the whims of memory and the procedure tends to be knowledge generating at least as much as knowledge testing. As such, it is a much more natural progression from the distance-learning phase and much more in keeping with the tone and texture of the course experience as a whole

Learner profile

This item of assessment requires course members in effect to carry out a small-scale linguistic research project that culminates in the writing of a performance analysis of an EFL learner. It thus provides a unique opportunity to critically evaluate input from the distance-learning and direct-contact phases and to begin to apply the insights gained to a real learner and their learning. The task includes a useful 'problem-solving' dimension, in that, on the basis of their data collection and analysis, course members are also invited to plan and implement a short series of one-to-one lessons. This provides a natural 'bridge' with the in-course teaching experience, thereby contributing to the internal coherence and cohesion of the course.

Materials compilation project

This is a further example of a process-orientated approach to in-course assessment. Its aim is to encourage autonomy and principled choice in the selection and preparation of learning materials. As with the learner profile, this project provides opportunities for the 'cumulative' application of insights from both phases of the course. The compilation is linked to the series of teaching events that course participants undertake and consists of a guided journal backed up by an actual collection of the visual aids, handouts, realia etc. used in each lesson. Journal entries are made at two points in time for each teaching event: the first, predictively, before the actual execution of the lesson and the second, reflectively, after it.

As the compilation proceeds, the choices made on various levels are naturally conditioned by learner reactions and subsequent decisions are better informed. The fact that teacher and learner reactions are recorded throughout in the form of a materials journal helps to ensure that in-course assessment has an important contribution to make to the process of personal and professional development.

Conclusion

All of the above and other features of the direct contact phase, then, complement the processes started in distance-learning mode. In this way distance-learning phase and direct-contact phase are seen as two complementary and, indeed, inseparable parts of a homogeneous educational experience. Either element, on its own, would prove less satisfactory than the combination of the two, and though no doubt the varied contexts in which teacher education takes place around the globe will mean that a choice occasionally has to be made between one mode and the other it is the experience of the writers that this frequently leads to a less than satisfactory outcome. If forced, we can all choose between strawberries and cream but we would hardly see one as an alternative to the other and most people would see the benefit of combining the flavours.

Notes

1. The use of the term 'training' in the title is designed to make the paper more accessible and its subject clearer to an audience that has grown up with the term — for a justification of the replacement term 'education', see p. 78.
2. One symptom of these trends in Sheffield is the abandonment of some slightly obsolete terminology. 'Controlled practice', for example, has been abandoned in favour of 'secure rehearsal', in other words providing learners with risk-free opportunities to manipulate newly and probably partially acquired language *before* it can be subjected to public scrutiny, evaluation and possibly criticism.

References

Bartlett, L. (1990) *Teacher Development Through Reflective Teaching.* In Richards, J. and Nunan, D. (eds) (1990): 202–214.

Richards, J. and Nunan, D. (eds) (1990) *Second Language Teacher Education.* Cambridge: Cambridge University Press.

Wallace, M. (1991) *Training Foreign Language Teachers: A Reflective Approach.* Cambridge: Cambridge University Press.

Widdowson, H. (1990) *Aspects of Language Teaching.* Oxford: Oxford University Press.

Appendix 6.1: Syllabuses for language awareness and phonology

Language awareness

Prescriptive *vs* descriptive views of language
Appropriacy of language
Word classes:

> open *vs* closed class items
> adjectives
> adverbs (manner/place/time/frequency/degree)
> conjunctions (co-ordinating/subordinating)
> determiners (pre-/central/post-)
> interjections
> nouns (uncountable/countable/abstract/concrete/proper) pro-
> > forms (personal/reflexive/possessive/interrogative/relative/
> > demonstrative/quantifying)
> verbs (lexical — transitive/intransitive, auxiliary-primary/modal)

Morphemes:

> definition/identification
> bound *vs* free morphemes
> roots *vs* affixes
> prefixes *vs* suffixes
> inflexional *vs* derivational affixes
> form/function anomalies with affixes
> word formation

Allomorphs of morphemes
Transparency *vs* opacity
Noun phrases
Pre- and post-modification
Relative clauses
Non-finite clauses
Prepositional phrases
Adjectival phrases
Verb Phrases:

> single item VPs
> complex VPs:
> > involving modals
> > involving perfectives
> > involving progressives
> > involving passives

operators in VPs:
> to mark tense
> to indicate question forms
> to attach negative markers
> for contrastive stress
> to form question tags

Dummy operator
Semantics and vocabulary
Semantic field theory
Componential analysis
Language functions

Phonology/phonemics and phonetics

Phonology

> Teachers' interest in learners' pronunciation
> Fluency and accuracy in the context of pronunciation
> Degrees of intelligibility
> Accent
> Prioritising phonological objectives
> Suprasegmental phonology
> The syllable
> Stress and the syllable
> Intonation groups
> Word-stress
> Contrastive stress
> Stress-timing
> Primary and secondary stress
> Splitting syllables
> Content and function words
> Phonological consequences of stress timing
> Strong and weak forms in spoken English
> Types of intonation pattern:
> fall/rise/rise-fall/fall-rise
> Nuclear stress at a syntactic level
> Nuclear stress at a semantic level

Phonemics

> Mismatch between sound and spelling
> Synchronic *vs* diachronic views of language
> Phoneme theory
> Language specificity of phoneme sets

Consonants and vowels
Phonemic symbols
Voiced *vs* voiceless sounds
Syllabic consonants
Articulation and the vowel
Cardinal vowels and their production
Classification of vowels
Diphthongs
Triphthongs
Articulation of:

plosives
fricatives
affricates
nasals
lateral /l/
frictionless continuants

Fortis *vs* lenis consonant sounds
Phonemic transcription

Phonetics and specific features

Complementary distribution
Allophones
Assimilation
Elision
Linkage

Appendix 6.2: Syllabus for pedagogical concerns and procedural skills

Background reading unit

Types of classroom interaction:

> closed
> open
> mixed

Classroom techniques:

> blackboard/whiteboard use
> OHP use
> video use
> cassette player use

Classroom management:

> pair-work
> group work
> individual work

Exploiting written material
Exploiting aural material
Developing skills:

> reading
> writing
> listening
> speaking

Evaluating learners' performance and progress
Teaching grammar points
Effective lesson planning
Developing course programmes
Evaluating types of material
Using pictures and mime
Elicitation techniques
Using non-linear text
Teaching children
Classroom language
Error correction techniques
Interactive roles of teacher and learner

7 Distance Education for Language Teachers and Educational Technology

GARY MOTTERAM

Introduction

The first part of this chapter will consider some of the problems of trying to teach educational technology for English Language Teaching (ELT) as part of a distance-education programme; the second part will consider the role of educational technology in the delivery of other ELT subjects taught at a distance. The term educational technology is used in a very narrow sense in the paper and refers only to the use of computers.

Educational technology in the form of television, radio, video and audio cassettes has been used for many years for the delivery of distance-learning materials, but it is only relatively recently that mainstream distance education institutions like the Open University (OU) have made use of computers as part of their range of tools for delivery of the curriculum. Computer-based learning is now becoming an increasingly important part of OU courses in all subject areas. In the field of ELT, distance education has helped us to challenge our accepted methods of teaching and shown us that technology has enormous potential in providing our clients with a considerably enhanced product.

The main concern of this paper will be Computer Assisted Language Learning (CALL). This is now a mainstream topic in the education of English language teachers. There are already four specialist master's courses that put technology in language teaching at the centre of their curriculum, while most diploma and master's level courses offer options in the subject, and British Council Specialist Schools are regularly devoted to it.

Teaching Educational Technology at a Distance

Language teacher education at a distance: the Manchester M.Ed. programmes

The course for which I am responsible in Manchester is the M.Ed. in Educational Technology and TESOL. This is a separate degree from the M.Ed. in Teaching English to Speakers of Other Languages (TESOL), but some modules are common to both. Students who are registered for the M.Ed. in Educational Technology and TESOL currently do six modules in total, four that cover the field of educational technology and ELT, and two others. They must also do a dissertation that relates educational technology and ELT. Both M.Ed. programmes are available in face-to-face and distance modes, although in practice all distance students do a part of the course face-to-face. In this paper, I describe one of the modules, the CALL module, developed for the distance learning version of the Ed. Tech. and TESOL course. For a more detailed discussion of aspects of the course see Motteram (1992).

The CALL module

A typical module in the face-to-face courses at Manchester consists of 10 sessions of two and a half hours; there is additional time for self-study and time allotted for an assignment. In distance materials this is normally paralleled by having an introductory unit 0, followed by 10 units of work covering the core content for the module.

The basic structure of the CALL module is as follows:

Unit 0	Introduction
Unit 1	Introduction to CALL/CBL/CML
Unit 2	Introduction to BBC/Macintosh/IBM compatible (according to need/choice)

followed by a choice of two from the following five topic options:

CALIS[1] (IBM)	4 units
HyperCard[2]	4 units (disk only)
Microtext[3] (BBC)	4 units
Microtext (IBM)	4 units
Guide[4]	4 units (some disk-based material).

On both the face-to-face and distance courses, students can potentially write software in any of four authoring packages: Computer Assisted Language Instruction System (CALIS), HyperCard, Microtext, and Guide, which is the software being used to produce the teacher-training materials discussed below.

The CALL distance module tries to follow the basic structure of other distance modules at Manchester, but needs to be more flexible to allow for differing student needs with regard to equipment.

The philosophy of the module is to provide an insight into authoring languages so that students can:

- write their own software if they feel the need;
- relate to what is going on in a team project for software creation and provide a valuable input;
- build up a greater knowledge of the field of CALL in general and have a more critical awareness of software and what can be done with it.

The materials themselves are divided into small sections containing relevant activities, and reference is made to the appropriate sections of the manual or any other books/articles as required. The first part of the module consists of an introduction to CALL; this is then followed by a review of software that has been written by other people (mainly previous students). These examples of software show the potential of the authoring languages themselves and act as reference points when students are trying to produce their own software as an assignment. Other sections focus on the authoring of software and follow very closely the work that is done in the face-to face teaching. Learning is checked through Self-Assessment Questions (SAQs) with a key in the back of the booklet, and Tutor-Assessed Questions (TAQs), which are marked either while the students are following the course or at the end. Students also have the option of sending their SAQ work to the tutor to be checked on a monthly basis.

One of the biggest problems in designing a course of this type is meeting the needs of a diverse clientele, particularly with respect to face validity. When the course started the main machine that was used to deliver it was the BBC B+. It was quickly realised that to satisfy the needs of the overseas learners at least some of the teaching would have to be done on IBM compatibles and luckily the Education Faculty was moving in that direction. There is also, increasingly, a need to use Macintosh computers in the delivery of material.

As anybody who has ever used a computer before knows there is no such thing as real compatibility between systems. IBM compatibles are the worst for this, but there are difficulties now with Macintoshes with the differences between System 6 and System 7. It is imperative to get as much information as possible from the students at the time that they register for their course, but inevitably there are difficulties as some students are not very familiar with what they are doing and may well be trying to use the module as an introduction to the field of CALL, which is not really what was intended.

My own attempts to provide a very wide range of choice has meant considerably more work and has left me with a complex administrative system. Students choose only two of the five options, but the tutor has to provide the extra range of units, and in addition the despatch of disks and the provision of support also increase the workload. I would certainly recommend that anyone thinking of writing a similar course think hard about whether they need it to run on more than one system.

Although a general introductory module on Educational Technology for ELT is proving very popular, the numbers of students following the CALL module at a distance at the moment is quite low. One of the difficulties the students face is getting feedback when something has gone wrong. This is particularly true for students who are not very familiar with computers in general. We have used e-mail and faxes to solve problems[5]; we have also tried to put the distance students in contact with students following the course face-to-face. What distance students cannot know is that face-to-face students only have access to tutors when they are in class, it is usually when the tutor leaves the room that the software that they are writing fails to work and they are forced to rely on their own notes. Distance students have a carefully designed booklet that has been trialled and rewritten on the basis of student feedback to help them with their work.

The students learn a considerable amount from the practical hands-on approach adopted in the CALL module. Most of them have access to a PC either at work or at home, and since it is increasingly an anticipation from employers that ELT teachers have a background and a competency in using computers with their learners, doing a module concerned with computing is, therefore, seen by most students as a vital part of a modern M.Ed. course.

This brings me to the second part of this chapter.

Using Technology to Deliver Distance Education

To date, most of the instructional materials in the CALL distance module are print-based, with authoring packages and examples of software supplied on disk. However, part of the module is delivered using Computer-Based Learning (CBL). Computer-Based Learning is becoming more and more common; it is the mother field for our own ELT CALL. The rest of this paper looks at the part of the CALL module that uses CBL techniques and considers ways in which similar techniques could be used to teach other aspects of ELT.

As was seen above, one of the topic areas in the CALL distance module involves HyperCard. This is a very versatile authoring language that is used by considerable numbers of educational and other institutions for delivering computer-assisted learning. There are a growing number of applications available in the language area as well. As the need to write the set of CALL units increased, Manchester University bought a site licence for Guide, a hypertext[6]-based authoring system. This is available on both Macintosh and IBM compatible machines. One of the inherent features of Guide is that it is able to 'launch' (a Guide metaphor) other pieces of software for demonstration purposes. (See Boyle, 1990 for work being done at Manchester Metropolitan University in the teaching of a computer language (Modula-2) to undergraduates.) This has meant that it has been possible to develop a unit of material (equivalent to four traditional units) to teach students how to make use of HyperCard in ELT. The material comes on one high density or two low density disks and the students can then transfer the package to a 'folder' on their hard disk. There will also be some print material to explain how the system works. An example of teaching material is provided and a second piece is put together as part of the training.

The sample screens below show how a module works. Figure 7.1 shows the 'folder' from which the module is launched and the way the material is built up in various blocks. Print material helps the student know where to start and how to continue to move about. There is a Welcome to Guide and this takes the user through the basics of navigating in a hypertext system. Figure 7.2 shows the buttons that are used to move from one part of the unit to the next. Figure 7.3 shows some of the text and graphics that are incorporated into the module. It is possible with the right machinery to have sound and moving pictures as well.

The Future

Guide is a very versatile package, firstly, because it runs on both IBM compatibles and Macintoshes and secondly, because it will launch other software. The next step will be to translate the whole of the existing distance CALL module into computer-based learning. It will certainly be possible to try out computer-based versions of at least some of the materials with next year's batch of full-time students. There are, however,

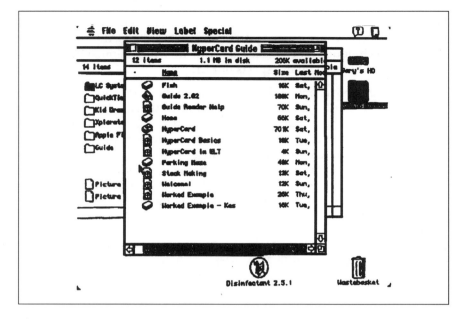

Figure 7.1

Figure 7.2

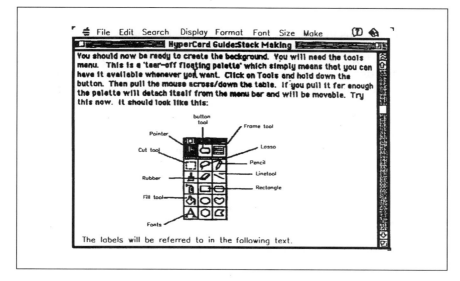

Figure 7.3

limitations as current versions of Guide will only run with Windows and not all of our students have machines capable of running Windows.

There have over the years been a number of attempts to create computer-based tests as part of the ELT field — the Edinburgh Placement Test (Hill, 1990), for example. As part of the Manchester module on Assessment, which is again currently only paper-based, we should be able to provide one unit that will demonstrate such computer-based tests.

This sort of material is an increasingly important part of the field of ELT in general. Distance materials are made more flexible by using technology. Experiences that are usually only possible to face-to-face students are made available to distance ones too. Many students can no longer afford to take a year off from their work in order to pursue a master's degree, but by providing a wide range of possibilities in the distance material students may make a choice about what they want to study and what technology they want to use: they can experience computer-based distance learning, paper-based or a mixture of the two. If they choose to take a mixture, students will have a broader range of experiences as part of their course. Students want to learn about technology and its relevance to language learning, even if only to confirm their own prejudices (and this is a very small percentage). Courses that fail to provide this vital element are failing their students at this level.

The next stage of our course development will be to begin working towards the delivery of the material in a composite form on CD ROM. It is my belief that in two years CD ROMs will be fitted as standard to most IBM compatible and Macintosh machines. With their large capacity and developing ability to integrate sound, text, animation, still and moving pictures they will be the obvious delivery mechanism for the kind of mixed media package that so much of our work in ELT requires.

It is hoped that from Summer 1994 we will begin working on the development of multimedia versions of a number of our materials. Again, the option will be there for people to follow such a course in a more traditional way using video and print material, but the ultimate aim is to deliver a whole module on CD ROM. Along with this will go other technological elements like e-mail and satellite. In other training and educational environments this is becoming standard practice. Why not in ELT?

Notes

1. The Computer Assisted Language Instruction System (CALIS) is shareware and is distributed by Duke University in the US.
2. HyperCard is a Macintosh program that comes as part of the system software and is used throughout the education world for the design of training materials.
3. Microtext was originally produced by the National Physical Laboratory and is distributed by Acorn for the BBC and until very recently by Distance Learning Systems for IBM compatibles. Carter (1988) has a training manual for this software published by the National Extension College.
4. Guide is published by OWL and is a hypertext authoring system (see note 6) available both for IBM compatibles running under DOS or Windows and for the Macintosh.
5. There is a small-scale research project currently going on looking at the value that e-mail can have in enabling students who are working at a distance to feel that they are in closer contact with their tutor. We are expecting to make further use of these support systems as the courses develop.
6. Hypertext is a term coined by an American, Ted Nelson. The idea is that as ideas are not developed in a linear way, then reading texts need not be presented in a linear way either. A hypertext system allows you to read material in any way you like. It also provides help and development issues on the way. You can usually trace where you have been to at the same time.

References

Boyle, T. (1990) The CORE approach to developing learning environments for programming. *Monitor* 1(1), 7–10. CTI Centre for Computing.

Carter, R. (1988) *CBT Programming in MICROTEXT.* National Extension College.

Hill, R. (1990) ToPE: *Test of Proficiency in English* (designed in collaboration with S. Fenn, Anglo World Education). University of Edinburgh.

Motteram, G. (1992) Authoring tools and teacher training for CALL. *System* 20(2), 151–60.

8 Virtual Language Schools: Overcoming the Problem of Distance in the Training of Language Teachers

J.C.H. JENNINGS

Introduction

Telematic technologies (the integration of computers and telecommunication systems) have recently been realised as powerful tools for the enhancement of distance education in general, and for distance teacher training in particular.

The group-based nature of some of these telematic systems makes them ideally suited to underpin the delivery of distance teaching where the communication between learners and their peers, as well as that between learners and their tutors, plays an important part in the process of education.

Within the domain of language teaching, these technologies provide learners with direct access to native-speakers across national boundaries. Students and teachers can work free from the constraints of time and distance (significant barriers to be overcome in distance education), and telematics can provide valuable support structures for the development of individual language skills and for the acquisition of those pedagogical techniques that are required for effective language teaching.

This chapter examines the organisational and technical requirements for the delivery of telematics-based courses in 'virtual language schools'. It describes the implementation of group-based telematics for training language teachers in preparation for the delivery of a pan-European language course within the Multimedia Teleschool. The Multimedia

Teleschool is a large-scale pilot project running under the European Community's DELTA (Developing European Learning through Technological Advance) programme.

Interactivity and Distance Teaching

Traditional distance-learning systems have been designed around the learning isolate, an individual learner who generally works by him- or herself and has communication links with his or her tutor through the postal and telephone systems (and, more recently, through fax machines). A typical isolated learner has few, if any, communication links with other learners. Early exponents of distance education, such as the UK Open University, soon realised the importance of tutor–student and student–student interaction in the educational process and, being aware this element was lacking in their first distance courses, instituted local and regional study centre systems to provide the facility for these interactions to take place.

Learning is best viewed as an active, co-operative and social process (Beckwith, 1983; Bruner, 1986; Davies, 1988) and, in that social context, the level and type of interaction between learners and teachers is an important factor in determining the effectiveness of learning.

In the provision of courses for language teachers, where communication is not only the means, but the end objective as well, the level and richness of interactivity that is provided within the structure of a course becomes a critical factor in the effective acquisition both of language skills, and of the pedagogical principles for effectively imparting those skills.

In distance education scenarios the social component of learning (the person–person interactivity) is often lacking. Tutor–student and, particularly, student–student communication is limited due to constraints of distance. For the delivery of courses whose primary aim is to develop communication skills so that successful students can teach communication through language, the absence of interactivity is a severe limitation. Distance students need to interact with their teachers and peers as much as students following face-to-face courses. The full richness of a distance-learning experience can only be achieved if some significant level of social interactivity is possible.

Advanced communication technologies offer the means to provide distance learners with access to a range of social environments where human interaction can take place. These technologies allow educationalists to construct group-oriented learning environments, permitting a full range of interaction between teachers and students, and particularly between students and students, to take place.

It is in this context that the Multimedia Teleschool has been established. It is designed to be a large-scale pilot project, delivering courses to students from a range of organisations across Europe using these new communication technologies linked to computer-based systems. The Multimedia Teleschool delivers telematics-based education — distance education with real interactivity.

The Berlitz 'English for Banking' Course

The Berlitz School of Languages has traditionally provided language courses for specific employment sectors. Berlitz courses are delivered 'in context'. The School does not provide a generic course in English, but relates the language syllabus to the students' working environment. Thus Berlitz has developed a number of English language courses for different market sectors, such as banking and telecommunications.

Standard Course Delivery Model

Traditionally, Berlitz distance language courses are delivered in a structured format involving modules based on four specific steps (processes).

(1) Background materials (paper-based and audio) are sent to the distant student prior to the start of the course.
(2) A study letter is sent, by post, from a personal tutor to the student. This study letter contains a personal letter and a series of directed assignments linked to the background materials.
(3) The student works on the assignments with the aid of the background materials and returns the completed work to the tutor through the postal system at the end of a two-week period.
(4) The tutor assesses the student's work and returns it along with the next study letter.

This standard distance-learning model provides only limited interaction between the student and tutor, and no interaction between one student and any of his peers. The student learns in relative isolation.

The Multimedia Teleschool Delivery Model

Seeing the limitations of the Standard Delivery Model at a time when Berlitz had come to an agreement to provide language courses for many banks in the East of the newly unified Germany, the company (along with a number of other commercial and academic organisations) received funding from the Commission of European Communities to establish 'The Multimedia Teleschool'. Using new communication technologies, the Multimedia Teleschool was designed to allow educational establishments to deliver fully interactive distance education. The isolated distance learner, within the Multimedia Teleschool, was to be an object of the past.

The Multimedia Teleschool model adopted by Berlitz has retained the four steps of the traditional courses, but includes a number of other elements:

(1) Background materials (paper-based and audio) are sent to the distant student by post, as in the standard course.

(2) A study letter is placed on one of the computer conferencing hosts by the tutor. The student connects to this computer from his own PC and retrieves the study letter.

(3) The student works on the assignments with the aid of the background materials. At two-week intervals a live one-hour satellite broadcast takes place in which various language acquisition activities and interviews with banking specialists occur. Students, situated in their study centres around Europe, are encouraged to interact with the tutors and guests in the television studio via a number of communication routes including telephone, facsimile, e-mail, computer conferencing and various video links (video-telephones). A number of competitive and collaborative activities are initiated by tutors during the broadcasts. In the period between broadcasts the student carries out various follow-up and group-based activities within the distributed computer conferencing system and completes the study letter (often with interactive support from his or her tutor or fellow students within the electronic environment). He or she then returns the completed work to his or her tutor in a private e-mail message to that tutor.

(4) The tutor assesses the student's work and returns it by e-mail. The student retrieves the next study letter from the host computer.

(See Appendix 8.1 for a sample of interaction taken from the Berlitz course.)

The implications for the distance teachers in the Multimedia Teleschool

Distance education teachers, inevitably, possess a different set of skills and techniques than teachers who work in face-to-face situations with their students. The interactivity which the Multimedia Teleschool model makes available to teachers and students lies closer to the face-to-face model than the traditional distance model. Levinson (1990) argues this for computer conferencing based education in general.

Berlitz distance-language teachers are used to teaching in an environment where they have very little contact with their students. The Multimedia Teleschool model requires them to lead and direct the learning of their students almost as if they were teaching them face-to-face. For the tutors to effectively implement this model they need not only to adapt to a different pedagogical approach, but to come to terms with a complex set of technologies as well.

Following analysis of the Standard Course Delivery model and the Multimedia Teleschool Delivery model (Davies, 1992), it was clear that a training course was necessary for the teachers.

Training the Teachers: The Berlitz Tutor Training Programme

Initial tutor training course

During development, and prior to delivery of the first 'English for Banking' course within the Multimedia Teleschool, a language teachers' training course was developed and delivered in order to assist tutors to acquire two basic sets of skills which they need:

(1) an understanding of, and familiarity with, the technological tools that they were to use;
(2) an appreciation of the range of pedagogical techniques that would be applicable when teaching within their new telematic environment.

Teacher training for the Berlitz Multimedia Teleschool was achieved in two ways:

(1) Attendance at a two-day face-to-face session where the technologies were explained and the tutors were given the opportunity to discuss, in a structured way, their existing pedagogies and the appropriateness of these for implementation within telematic environments. The possibilities of adapting current teaching methods to the new delivery mode were examined. Strategies were worked out by tutors, with the assistance of telematics specialists, for the telematic delivery of the courses.

(2)   The face-to-face session was followed by a four-week structured on-
      line course that offered the tutors a range of activities and a forum to
      discuss their individual ideas regarding the methodologies to be
      used in delivering their courses. Activities included a series of
      familiarisation exercises, giving the teachers time to become
      comfortable with the technology and to address any problems they
      might encounter in using a modem and remotely logging into a host
      computer. The familiarisation exercises were followed by weekly
      modules that were designed to introduce them to the computer-
      conferencing environment and to teach them how to manage groups
      of students within it.

At the end of this teacher training course each participant delivered a
practice lesson to the group.

It is important that teachers who come fresh to using new technologies,
and to teaching with these new technologies, first experience the learning
environment as a student. It is only by assuming the role of students that
the teachers can appreciate some of the initial apprehension and
confusion that is quite common when people find themselves in new
learning situations. Individually, the tutors develop strategies to manage
their learning within their telematic world and, in so doing, develop a
deeper understanding of their students' requirements in the initial,
sometimes difficult, stages of their courses.

Tutor support structures

In parallel with the tutor training course, tutors were introduced to
fully configured Microsoft Windows software tools. These included
communications software and a 'learning network management' software
tool that provided tutors with detailed analysis of student activity within
the computer conferencing and e-mail system at any point in time.

Technical staff in the Berlitz offices were actively encouraged to become
involved in the installation of communications equipment and in
exploring the nature of the teaching and learning environment so that
they could provide a high level of support to all participants whenever it
was needed.

Overcoming the Problems of Teaching Interactively at a Distance

Within the 'English for Banking' course group interaction occurs in two
ways:

- synchronously during the direct broadcast by satellite (DBS) sessions. Students use feedback links to the studio for tutor–student communication (often more than one tutor and one student are involved in the interactions);
- asynchronously within the computer-mediated communication system (the e-mail and conferencing environment) throughout the duration of the course.

Problems with synchronous interaction

Synchronous group interaction raises few communication issues for tutors and students, as the mix of broadcast television and telephone/video feedback loops fits well within standard conceptual structures that all participants have previously encountered. We all operate within synchronous environments in our daily lives. The added layer of technology may cause problems in itself initially, but these are usually transitory.

Problems with asynchronous interaction

The asynchronous communication systems, however, pose several communication and conceptual problems for many participants. People used to working within 'real' educational environments constructed from bricks and mortar find navigation through an essentially 'flat' digital environment where interaction does not occur in real-time somewhat difficult. Computer environments traditionally lack sufficient location and navigation cues and the very real problem of disorientation is commonplace. A Learning Network Design methodology has been developed (Davies, 1989) to assist with the construction of virtual organisations so that all participants working within these 'virtual worlds' can make sense of their environment, navigate through it, and learn effectively within it.

Visual metaphors

As part of the Learning Network Design methodology a visual metaphor (Figure 8.1) is developed with course designers and teachers to act as an aid for all participants and to ease some of the navigational problems which are encountered due to the lack of visual cues within current computer networks.

Each tutor and each student has a paper copy of his or her 'Language Learning Centre' that they can use as a navigational aid. Feedback from participants suggests that this simple tool offers great help, particularly in the early stages of a course.

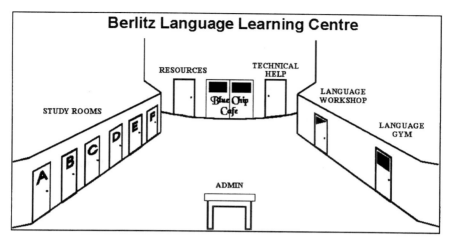

Figure 8.1 The Berlitz European Language Learning Centre

Tightly structured courses

One of the essential elements in telematics-based course design and delivery is the way in which the course is structured. Teachers have found that careful design of activities and their close monitoring makes for a higher level of discourse and, through the discourse, more effective learning.

The Berlitz tutors found that their teaching proved most effective when they provided an environment based upon a mix of small-group seminars, led by a single tutor, and large group discussion and case study work led by a number of tutors working collaboratively. One problem encountered was that some of the small seminar-type groups were not as actively involved in their group work as others. This is not unusual in normal face-to-face teaching situations either. In these cases an even more structured pedagogy was used, including regular private communication with the individuals in the group (through e-mail) encouraging them to become active participants in the learning process through group work.

Becoming comfortable with the technology

The initial teacher-training course gave the tutors both the experience of learning within a telematic environment themselves and also removed many of the apprehensions that they may have had regarding the technology. At the time the teacher-training course was carried out (late

1992) computer conferencing systems could still sometimes be technologically hostile. Although much effort was put into the development of easy-to-use communications software and simple interfaces to the conferencing host, participants need both time and comprehensive support in order to become comfortable in such complex environments. By the end of the eight-week teacher training course, all tutors were familiar with the basic functions of the systems and were able to participate effectively in private and public electronic discussions.

General Organisational and Technical Requirements for Telematics-based Distance Teaching

The experience gained in delivering the Berlitz courses, and in work with other organisations providing telematics-based distance courses, has allowed the identification of two issues which are key to the effective delivery of such courses:

- organisational issues;
- technical issues.

Organisational issues

Distance Education has developed as a viable teaching/learning scenario within educational organisations. However, in many cases, organisational structures and systems have lagged behind the range of possibilities in telematics-based distance teaching. Large educational organisations suffer from inertia in the same way other large organisations do. There are many barriers to the introduction of courses designed so that students rarely, if ever, are physically on campus, where there is little need for teachers to be on campus for much of the time, and where teachers do not necessarily have to be located in close proximity to the educational establishment. In the case of the Berlitz course described, the tutors are, in fact, located at a specialist centre some 20 km away from the main administrative centre, but the tutors could, without adverse effect, be located anywhere in Europe.

There can be no doubt that two factors will assume increasing importance for educational organisations through and beyond the last part of this century:

(1) The requirement for the provision of distance education will increase in response to the increasing difficulty that those in employment have attending 'traditional' part-time courses, the increasing mobility of populations, and the increasingly dynamic nature of many organisational structures.

(2) Rapid advances in telecommunications will make more sophisticated technology available more widely at lower cost. These technologies will provide the communication tools on which to build the distance education programmes of the future.

If telematics-based education is to be implemented successfully to take advantage of these two factors, it is important that the organisational infrastructure is fully prepared for the changes that will come with it. Unless the university, faculty, department or company preparing to implement telematics-based courses is prepared to analyse the organisational changes required for this new mode of educational delivery, and to take action to ensure that organisational infrastructure supports (rather than inhibits) such delivery, it will not be fully successful.

Technical issues

Individual technologies, by themselves, fall short in providing complete solutions. Provision of a fully featured learning environment for distributed learners requires the careful integration of a number of technological components in a seamless manner.

Despite the limitations of the various technologies, through careful planning in pedagogical design and integration of existing communication technologies, together with the focused development of a range of technical systems, it is possible for a coherent provision to be made that will offer all the tools required for the delivery of fully featured telematic distance education.

Of importance to future distance teacher training programmes is the development of broad band telecommunication networks, which will allow the transfer of large amounts of data in acceptable time scales, the development of voice-annotated text and voice-annotated groupware tools, and the development of full multimedia communication networks that can offer a platform for rich communication forms including text, sound, voice, image, video and other multimedia elements.

Specific Requirements for Telematics-based Teaching

The Multimedia Teleschool has used a broad range of technological tools in the delivery of its courses. However, courses can be delivered using simple and less expensive telematic technologies.

E-mail systems

Interactivity can be introduced to course delivery by simply making an e-mail system available to all participants. There are many documented cases of the use of e-mail (Levin, Kim & Reil, 1990) to enhance distance learning. E-mail can be implemented easily and cheaply. There are a number of educational suppliers of e-mail systems and facilities in the UK if an organisation does not want to set up and maintain its own system for distance students. Most e-mail software used on Local Area Networks can be configured for dial-in access from remote sites. The costs involved to establish such a system include a modem for each remote user — prices of modems are rapidly falling and one can be purchased in the UK for about £50–80; appropriate communications software, which can often be obtained free; and the cost of the telephone connections, along with initial set-up costs.

Group-based systems

Group-based systems (usually referred to as computer conferencing systems, or groupware) are also quite widely available now and can be relatively cheap to establish and run. Systems may cost as little as £500 to set up. However, there is usually an overhead in maintaining group-based systems and, although most university Information Technology centres have the expertise to establish conferencing hosts, it is important that regular maintenance of the conferencing system and network connections, and close support of users, is carried out. It is because of such issues that some course providers choose to make use of outside computer conferencing facilities where a small monthly fee is paid for each user and the facilities house provides all the software, communications connections and user support.

Interactive multimedia systems

Full interactive multimedia systems such as the Multimedia Teleschool are expensive to establish and run. Direct broadcast by satellite requires the use of costly television studios and the rental of time on satellites in addition to the range of terrestrial networks. Effective implementation of such systems currently is best carried out by consortia of organisations where expertise is spread throughout the group and large numbers of students can offset the high cost of delivery.

Conclusions

The delivery of the language courses, and the associated language teacher training programmes, for the Multimedia Teleschool, have effectively demonstrated the appropriateness of telematics-based distance education for such purposes.

However, a cautious and balanced approach to the introduction of telematics should be taken. Outcomes have shown that the technological issues are not necessarily the most difficult to overcome. Technology has not been shown to be a constant limiting factor. Organisational and pedagogical issues are of prime importance and the need for careful planning, preparation and teacher training continue to dominate, as they do in all forms of educational design.

Note

Multimedia Teleschool Project Partners involved in the 'English for Banking' course: Audio Visual Centre, University College Dublin; Berlitz, Frankfurt; CECOMM, Southampton Institute; Condat, Berlin; EUROSTEP, Leiden; France Telecom, Montpellier; GATE-UPM, Madrid; IET, Thessaloniki; Katholieke Universiteit, Leuven; La Sept, Paris; University College, London; Wissenschaftliches Institut für Kommunikationsdientse, Bad Honnef.

References

Beckwith, D. (1983) The nature of learners as total systems with implications for research and instructional development: A theoretical/conceptual paradigm. *Journal of Visual Verbal Languaging* Autumn 1983: 9–28.

Bruner, J. (1986) *Actual Minds, Possible Worlds.* Cambridge, MA: Harvard University.

Davies, D. (1988) Computer-supported cooperative learning systems. *Programmed Learning and Educational Technology* 25(3), 205–215.

Davies, D. (1989) Learning network design: Coordinating group interaction in formal learning environments over time and distance. Paper delivered at NATO Advanced Seminar on Computer Supported Learning. Maratea, Italy, October.

Davies, D. (1992) *The Multimedia Teleschool: Functionalities and Pedagogic Scenarios.* Brussels: Delta Project 2021 Report, CEC DG XIII.

Harasim, L. (ed.) (1990) *Online Education: Perspectives on a New Environment.* New York: Praeger.

Levin, J., Kim, H. and Reil, M. (1990) Analysing instructional interactions on electronic message networks. In Harasim, L. (ed.) (1990): 185–213.

Levinson, P. (1990) Computer conferencing in the context of the evolution of media. In Harasim, L. (ed.) (1990): 5–14.

Appendix 8.1 Extract of interaction taken from the Berlitz 'English for Banking' course

This extract demonstrates some of the techniques adopted by the tutors to teach language skills within a computer conference environment.

Comments

1. This electronic discussion about the use of the words 'opportunity' and 'possibility' was initiated by a tutor (Gerry Adams) as a new conference Item (or subject). He introduced some examples of the use of these two words and asked students to enter further examples to demonstrate their understanding of the words.
2. A student (Volker Krabbe) entered his response to the tutor's request.
3. The tutor then commented on the student's contribution and made suggestions for more appropriate use of the word 'join' which was used by the student.
4. A second tutor (Tara Smith) then added a further suggestion for use of the word 'join'.

Item 5

Opportunity

=== by Gerry Adams   16 Nov 92 07:47 GMT

Two words which are frequently used incorrectly are 'opportunity' and 'possibility'. As a very general tip, use the word 'opportunity' as you would 'chance'. Here are some examples:

Investors have the opportunity to invest in shares.

I'm sorry, but I didn't have the opportunity to call you.

Living in Frankfurt allows you the opportunity to visit the stock exchange.

I want to see some more examples entered by YOU now. Give three sentences, one in the past, one in the present and one in the future each using the word 'opportunity'.

12 Discussion responses

5:1) Volker Krabbe   16 Nov 92 08:58 GMT

I hope I'll have the opportunity to spend my next vacation in Canada.

I'm sorry, but I didn't have the opportunity to join the multimedia teleschool last week.

Do you have the opportunity to visit the 'Dom' of Cologne?

- — - — -

5:5) Gerry Adams   23 Nov 92 02:49 GMT

Volker, your use of 'opportunity' is good. When you are speaking about the teleschool, however, 'participate in' is better than 'join'. We use 'join' when we become a member of something for the first time.

- — - — -

5:6) Tara Smith   23 Nov 92 07:04 GMT

'Join' can also be used to mean 'meet'.

For example: I'll try to join you in the pub before eight o'clock.

                      He said he'd join us as soon as he'd finished work.

'Join in' also means 'take part in'.

For example: Everyone joined in with the dancing.

                      The more people who join in the gym exercises, the better!

- — - — -

Virtual Language Schools   7

9 Interaction Across Computer-Conferencing

CHRISTINA HOWELL-RICHARDSON

Introduction

The purpose of this chapter is to report on work in progress in research into group interaction across computer-conferencing on educational courses. This research will be of interest to language teacher educators, as computer conferencing is now being used in courses for language teachers, e.g. the MA TESOL by computer conferencing at the Institute of Education, University of London. (See also Jennings, Chapter 8.) The aim of the (Ph.D.) research is to investigate the social and communication processes of interaction in computer-conferencing for the purposes of identifying the conditions that affect student performance in collaborative learning activities. The research is based on observation of two sixteen-week courses in online training and education — a collaborative project between the Institute of Education, London University and the Open University. The experimental focus of this project was to compare the effects of different course-design features and pedagogical methods on group interaction.

The paper describes in general terms the primary features of interaction across computer-conferencing and outlines a preliminary descriptive model. Finally, the discussion takes up the implications of the model for the tutor's role in computer-mediated communication courses.

Defining Computer-mediated Communication

Computer-mediated communication (CMC) is one of a set of telecommunications media supporting multi-party verbal exchange. Specifically, CMC, which comprises computer-conferencing and electronic mail, supports asynchronous text-based communications. The focus of this chapter is computer-conferencing (as opposed to electronic mail) since conferencing systems can be used to provide a variety of structures for shared working areas unavailable within the dyadic communications structure of electronic mail and have a number of properties that are potentially well-adapted to suppport collaborative group activities (Kaye, 1992: 5).

Briefly, individual participants, using a local personal computer (PC), modem and communications software, access the conferencing system housed on a central host computer. The host supports a large number of conferences on specific subjects, each of which is usually further organised into a number of separate files. Within each conference the total communications as entered by the members of the conference are logged in chronological sequence (see Appendix 8.1 to Jennings, Chapter 8, for an example). Having connected to the conferencing system participants then have an option among a number of activities, for instance to read or send private mail; to read through new messages in the conferences of which they are members; to contribute messages or to scan through the conference transcripts using online search commands.

Computer access to interactive databases over networks and interactive, intelligent tutoring systems, which can also be used in 'stand-alone' mode, are now relatively familiar applications within education. However, the sense in which the term 'interactivity' is applied to computer conferencing differs significantly from these applications. In using databases and intelligent tutoring systems the participant (or participants if two or more learners use the software simultaneously) is engaged in interaction with the computer program. In computer-conferencing, on the other hand, as the interactant parties are the members of the conferencing group, the computer program merely acts as the medium for the exchange to take place.

The implications of this distinction are:

(1) CMC supports multi-party interaction in addition to multi-party communication, which could also be achieved using the carbon-copy facility available in electronic mail. The term 'multi-party' interaction is here used to imply that all participants have equal social and discourse rights. They are all equally the target addressee of an utterance and are equally sanctioned in the right to respond to a previous utterance or to initiate new topics.

(2) Although interaction via computer-conferencing has often been represented as time-independent (Harasim, 1990: 46), this is not the

case. As in any conversational exchange there are temporal constraints on response time and currency of debate. Within computer-conferencing these time-frames are extended but not unlimited.

'An Altered State of Communication'

(Johansen, Vallee & Spangler, 1979: 12)

Murray Turoff predicted that the defining features of his brainchild (computer conferencing) would result in changes in the psychology and sociology of the communication process itself. This prediction has been borne out, since these features determine the contextual, interpersonal and discourse conditions within which interaction occurs and thus a communications environment specific to CMC. The nature and impact of these conditions requires complex analysis. However, for the purposes of generality, they can be approximately described under four broad categories:

(1) configuration of conferencing environment;
(2) effects of reduction in social cues;
(3) effects of asynchronous text-based exchange;
(4) participant interaction strategies.

Configuration of conferencing environment

Conferencing software systems provide a number of options for the organisation of messages within a conference and for allocation of varying degrees of access rights to the conference as a whole or to the files within a conference. The design of a structure for a conference and the denotation of its different areas are analogous in purpose and effect to those of organisation structure for the management of human resources. The structure not only implicitly communicates a philosophical and social culture (Handy, 1987) but also establishes role-models for the participants and defines the route and purpose of communications pathways between participants.

Choice and denotation of structure are usually guided by the objectives of the communications task, e.g. the requirement for a restricted access work area for collaborative writing tasks in contrast to an open-access area for plenary discussion. Moreover, in CMC these structures are entirely flexible and can be easily re-configured to adapt to changes in participants' communications needs or if existing structures prove inappropriate. It is also possible to graft customised software structures onto existing systems to enhance particular objectives; for example a gateway that automatically bars learners from access to the tutorial group until they have entered their own answer to the question in discussion (Hiltz, 1986).

If the communications purposes implied by these structures are ambiguous or if the structure is inappropriate to the needs and objectives of the participants then some of the following problems may be observed: inappropriate verbal behaviour (Kiesler, Siegel & McGuire 1984); loss of participant motivation (Thomas, 1989); participant drop-out (Thorpe, 1989); loss of focus and lack of relevance in the discussion (Mason, 1989); process-loss, i.e difficulties in co-ordination of procedural activities (Kiesler, 1992).

Effects of reduction of social context cues

In CMC many of the paralinguistic and social cues relied upon to make inferences about the context, fellow participants and management of the interaction are filtered out. The most immediate effects of this ambiguity are firstly a reduction in conformity to certain of the pragmatic constraints that guide face-to-face (FtF) interaction and secondly greater opportunity for equality of participation, which is particularly beneficial to minorities, the disabled and women, who are often not encouraged by the traditional classroom environment to actively participate.

With respect to a reduction in pragmatic constraints there are three primary trends. Firstly, the obligation to respond to others is often weakened, partly due, in the absence of gaze, etc. to lack of speaker nomination of addressee(s) and partly due among some participants to an adverse reaction to asynchronicity, such that they will only engage in discussion if able and stimulated to do so immediately (Grint, 1989). But as this strategy is often at odds with the more reflective dynamics of recorded text-based communication, response rate can be suppressed. Secondly, certain politeness constraints are weakened, particularly those relating to avoidance of face-threatening illocutionary acts. Uninhibited interpersonal behaviour is not unknown in CMC groups (Siegel *et al.*, 1986; Spitzer, 1986) and can take the form of over-harsh reactions to others' comments ('flaming') or relatively unrestrained disclosure of personal attitudes and feelings. In CMC, silence is included within this concept:

> [But] silence can be both brutal and ambiguous. One can interpret it as complete rejection, or lack of understanding, or laziness, or equipment breakdown. In each case, the results are equally chilling (Spitzer, 1986: 20).

Conversely, a third impact of the reduction in social context cues and absence of paralinguistic expression is that utterances take on altered illocutionary effects. One explanation for this is transfer of verbal behaviour the appropriate interpretation of which in FtF interaction would be achieved through supplementary inferences made in phonological, paralinguistic, discourse and social-context domains; illocutionary modifications, which in CMC can only be communicated by an explicit statement of speaker intent. A second cause is the difficulty of gauging the appropriate level of shared knowledge between interlocutors. If too many assumptions are made about the degree of shared understanding, too much is left to reader-inference thereby limiting the likelihood of convergence between interlocutors. In FtF negotiation of shared meaning can be conducted fairly rapidly, and frequently relies on paralinguistic cues. In CMC, however, lack of proximity — both physical and temporal — and irregularities in participation rates and distribution can impede accuracy of judgements about one's audience.

The second immediate derivative of a reduction in social cues is more equal levels of participation and therefore lower probability of the emergence of a single dominant leader (Kerr & Hiltz, 1982; Rice & Associates, 1984). Bales' (1978) research indicates that, in FtF groups, signifiers of personal charisma such as voice-tone, physical appearance and speed in taking early initiatives are among the primary variables in predicting the identity of a group leader. The emergence of such a leader, once recognised and accepted by the group, is usually consistent with greater incidence of consensus and greater ease and speed in collaborative decision-making since the group, through the mediation of the leader, strive to avoid conflict and to converge on a single solution. Given that there is greater opportunity for divergent voicing of opinion and lower likelihood of individual dominance, it is hardly surprising that several studies have shown that CMC groups have difficulty in decision-making tasks (Kiesler, Siegel & McGuire, 1984; Siegel *et al.*, 1986) which in practice results in the higher incidence of process-loss in CMC groups.

Effects of asynchronous text-based exchange

CMC interaction differs significantly from other media in terms of the discourse structure and topic development and in the dynamics of turn-taking.

Turn-taking in CMC does not require the same social management skills as in FtF; there are no interruptions, no technical restrictions on the length of a message, and no social or technical impediments to contributing a string of messages in a sequence. Moreover, the convention of linking adjacent messages topically is relaxed. It is very common to find adjacent messages in the transcript that are not linked to each other at all — topically, referentially or inferentially. Nor are they intended to be linked. There is a good reason for this.

As group members log-on at different times and may have varying or unpredictable schedules for logging-on, it is common practice to comment on messages occurring much earlier in the transcript even if there are a large number of intervening messages on unrelated topics. This practice is carried out and supported in two different ways. Firstly, the CoSy software (the computer conferencing software used on the OU mainframe) automatically prompts a contributor to designate a message as free-standing (SAY response) or as commenting (COMMENT response) on a specified message. If the 'COMMENT' prompt is chosen the message is automatically linked by a hypertext-type link to the message specified and this information is marked in the message header. Secondly, many experienced CMC users take the extra precaution of reiterating the topic or main points of the originating message or source discussion, or use other explicit cohesive devices such as identifying the author and message number, in order to establish topical and referential links between messages.

It is for this reason that the discourse structure and patterns of topic development in CMC interaction are idiosyncratic to the medium. CMC discourse structure is most usually characterised by multiple parallel topic development and a reduction in coherence across utterances that are proximally related in favour of a more complex (frequently explicit) pattern of cohesion across an extended discourse domain.

However, the effect on the participant cannot automatically be estimated on the basis of CMC text as a product. The text as logged on the system exists in a state of duality. It is simultaneously both a product of the interaction and a transitional stage to be re-organised and reformulated by individual participants using offline software editing packages or techniques such as printing, cutting and pasting for filing in a document folder. What can be assumed, however, is that the need for editing and reformulation increases the overall study-load and this is confirmed by student feedback on a number of CMC courses (Harasim, 1987; Sorensen & Kaye, 1992). It can also be assumed that as each individual re-organises the text according to his/her own schematic framework this will have an impact on the process of group convergence on a shared frame for the discourse. (See above.)

Overload is also caused by unpredictability in the rate of messaging. It is impossible to estimate at any log-on session, even if logging-on within a matter of days or hours, the number and volume of accumulated unread messages. Overload is further exacerbated by multiple turn-taking particularly if the span of an individual's contribution requires cross-referencing to a number of earlier messages on disparate topics.

Participant interaction strategies

It will have now become clear that CMC interaction requires skills in social management and in information management which differ from those required in other communications media. The following description of three strategies in the domain of social management provides an illustration of the types of skills required:

- As already mentioned in the previous section one of the main characteristics of CMC discourse structure is a reduction in coherence across adjacent utterances. In compensation, the discourse is often marked by explicit cohesion. This is an intentional strategy, particularly among experienced users. Among the most commonly used cohesive devices are: reference to an earlier message by message number and contributor's name; placing of the topic sentence in initial position; a brief paraphrase of the status quo of the discussion in the opening paragraph of the message, or — even in comment messages — use of titles.
- Participants wishing to contribute messages to the conference have a choice of two modes: to immediately key in a message online or to prepare messages offline for transfer (uploading) to the conference. The advantages of uploading are the greater time permitted for reflection, cross-referencing to earlier messages and crafting of the text, which leads to higher quality educational interaction. On the other hand, just as in FtF, light, off-the-cuff or phatic comments facilitate group cohesion and therefore the process of debate. Skilful users are usually able to judge the appropriate use of light-hearted comments, which if misplaced may be interpreted as flippancy or 'flaming', or may simply exacerbate problems of coherence in CMC discourse.
- Learners also have a choice in mode of participation: to actively contribute messages or to follow the discussion by reading. Although this latter practice in the early days of CMC attracted the pejorative label 'lurking', these negative connotations have now largely been dropped. As a communications and learning strategy 'lurking' is a conscious decision not to actively contribute when

time (or other) pressures are such that active participation would make participation unsatisfactory or when one's subject knowledge is limited.

A Preliminary Model of CMC Group Interaction

The conditions affecting group interaction across CMC are numerous, complex and interacting. I have therefore attempted to identify a system of hyperordinates which will satisfy the following criteria:

(1) In combination these hyperordinates have descriptive value for the primary characteristics of CMC group interaction.

(2) Those conditions that are identified as affecting group interaction in CMC and that are specific to the medium can be subsumed under one, or more than one, of these hyperordinates.

(3) As it is representative of the conditions affecting CMC interaction, this system can be influenced by interaction with independent agents. Consequently, the actions of a tutor-moderator, or changes within the conferencing system or conferencing structure directed towards any of these hyperordinates will influence the conditions of interaction.

A system of hyperordinates

Four parameters are proposed as having descriptive and explanatory value for the conditions influencing group interaction across CMC, as described in the previous section. The primary constituent variables within each of these parameters are as follows:

Participation rate and distribution

This is the frequency with which individual members contribute messages and the proportionate number of group members contributing during a period of active debate. This parameter is hypothesised to relate chiefly to critical mass (achieving sufficient volume and breadth of debate to make the discussion viable); the extent to which participants are able to achieve convergence on a shared discourse framework, which is partly related to frequency of participation and continuity in active group membership; reduction in pragmatic constraints on response and response-times.

Group co-ordination and process-loss

This parameter is hypothesised to be related mainly, but not exclusively, to three sets of conditions. Firstly, to social–psychological conditions affecting group process, such as the conditions that give rise to more equality in participation and the suppression of individual dominance, which in turn lead to greater incidence of divergent voicing of opinion. Secondly, to the perceived effects of altered illocutionary value of utterances in CMC, which may for instance inhibit assertive behaviour or produce 'flaming', and that create difficulties in the interpretation of silence. Thirdly, two aspects of asynchronicity are relevant: extended overall task-time and the currency value of a proposal, which if not taken up within a critical period will usually be rejected by default.

Shared knowledge

The difficulties of attaining convergence on a shared discourse framework have already been briefly referred to. The hypothesis is that this parameter is primarily related to the unique structure of CMC discourse; to degree of learner skill in the management of information and intra-group behaviour; to the effects of a reduction of context cues provided within either the physical or co-temporal dimension (e.g. graphics in text, intonation in speech, gaze, etc.) and the incidence of greater divergence of opinion resulting from equal opportunities in rights of participation. Asynchronicity of exchange has significance in its own right in that time-lapses allow for more extended interpretive procedures that often result in greater displacement of the frame of discourse context between exchanges than would be the case in the immediacy of FtF, where pragmatic constraints of discourse coherence apply.

Information density (in terms of volume of information and the number and disparity of topics developed in parallel)

In principle, this parameter relates primarily to CMC discourse structure; CMC discourse strategies such as multiple turn-taking; group/individual procedures for messaging behaviour (e.g. use of cohesive links); and to temporal factors such as unpredictability in the rate and volume of messaging.

It is further argued, on the basis of participant observation of the two courses and a preliminary analysis of the data, that these four parameters are closely interacting. This also in turn predicts that changes in any one parameter will bring about associated changes within the other three. For instance, if in response to process-loss an authoritative person (the tutor–moderator or high status group member for example) is able to gain acceptance for a specific topic and set of task procedures, this not only partly delimits the possible range of divergence in schematic knowledge but also affects patterns of participation (either causing an increase or decrease in participation through topic focus and the manner in which it is achieved) and consequently levels of information density.

Asynchronicity, in the specific sense of a critical period for currency of debate and response time, is not only a defining feature of computer-conferencing but also occurs as a constituent variable within each parameter. Asynchronicity is therefore separated out in order to fully indicate its impact on all four parameters.

Influence of independent agents on the system of hyperordinates

The influence of independent agents is the third criterion for justification of the descriptive value of the model (criterion 3, p. 125). Two agents that are proposed for consideration to evaluate the fulfilment of this criterion are the tutor and the course design, including the structural configuration of the conferencing environment itself and the nature of the task.

For example, as argued above, the structural configuration of the conference is taken as one means to define communications pathways and can either contextualise or, if inappropriately configured, obscure the purposes of different conference areas. If this function operates in such a way that the pattern of participant activity alters and/or the relevance of accumulated messages to the topic within a conference is markedly affected then this gives support to the hypothesis that infrastructure interacts with and influences the system of hyperordinates proposed.

It is further proposed that intervention on the part of a tutor during the process of group interaction, whether direct intervention in terms of metacomment on group processes or indirect through for instance reconfiguration of infrastructures or use of the backchannel mode of private mail to interact with participants, affects the prevailing conditions of interaction. This aspect of the tutor's role and its relation to the four parameters proposed is discussed further in the next section. The model is presented diagrammatically in Figure 9.1.

Possible Implications of the Model for Tutor Role

Previous discussions of techniques for the facilitation of CMC groups have emphasised the roles of 'chairperson' (Brochet, 1985), to set an agenda and steer the discussion; editor (Feenburg, 1987), to summarise and interpret; and host (Carlson, 1986), to set the intellectual and emotional climate and to provide pastoral support. The model proposed, however, permits much greater specificity in defining the roles that might be required of the tutor–facilitator.

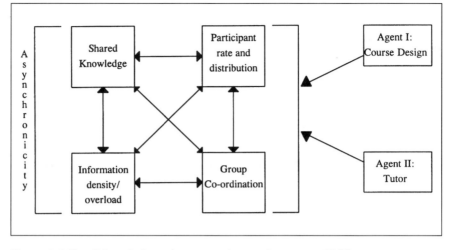

Figure 9.1 Conditions influencing group interaction across CMC

Within the confines of this chapter it is not possible to do more than to draw inferences from the model about what the predominant concerns of CMC group facilitation might be in addition to the tutor's role as instructor. These inferences suggest predominant concern with at least five aspects of course management:

Structuring of the environment and task design

A design for a conference structure can only be effective and efficient in providing an organisational and communications framework if there is seamless integration with the requirements of the task and the requirements of the participants. Therefore, analysis of the demands of the task in combination with analysis of the types of support structures required by a particular participant group to achieve their learning objectives predetermine the structural configuration of the conferencing environment.

Selection of task-type requires consideration of the special conditions of CMC, in particular extended task-time, the likelihood of process-loss and the greater difficulties of achieving convergence on a shared discourse framework. Participant attitude to the task is also relevant, given that in CMC participants do at times display uninhibited verbal behaviour and that motivation to actively contribute over an extended period is largely maintained through intrinsic interest in and satisfaction with the process of the discussion.

The primary constraint on the formation of a CMC group is size. Since the optimal use of computer-conferencing is multi-party interaction (cf. multi-party communication) with all that this entails for issues of shared knowledge and information density, group size should not exceed limits within which such interaction can take place — between six and twelve participants, depending upon predicted frequency of individual participation rates.

The competence level of the individual group members in relation to the task is a second major constraint on collaborative group work. A group of competent individuals often achieve a level of performance surpassing the sum of their individual abilities. Conversely, grouping of individuals who are incompetent in relation to the task results in a weaker performance than would be achieved by the individual member working alone (Tziner & Eden, 1985). Within CMC the nature of the competence required for collaborative work is multi-dimensional and comprises not only individual resources with respect to the task (as would be implied FtF) but also medium-specific skills in the social management of the interaction and cognitive skills in information management. However, the strength of the medium for supporting multi-party interaction can also be harnessed to exploit the strengths of non-homogeneous groups, whose individual members each have complementary skills in relation to the task. Depending on the objectives of the group, this may expedite task completion and/or promote peer-learning.

Formative evaluation

The structural configuration and denotation of conference areas, as described above, can be altered at any time. The technical authority to make these alterations lies in the hands of the convenor of the conference (known as the moderator), but this does not necessarily imply authority of decision-making. It is simple to implement an effective feedback loop through, for example, designation of a separate conference area for formative evaluation of the course. There is no practical impediment to making this area open-access to all those involved in the course, whether as participants, tutors, course designers, administrators, etc. Nor is there any practical impediment to collaborative decision-making concerning changes to course structure, content or focus being taken within this forum.

Editorial responsibilities

Editorial functions within CMC have previously been conceived as a combination of summarising functions and interpretive functions;

drawing together the threads of a discussion and reformulating them into a comprehensible sequence (Feenburg, 1987). But herein lies the difficulty, since the two functions have distinct propositional and illocutionary values, particularly if performed by a tutor.

Summarising of the discussion at regular intervals is clearly a requirement in order to crystallise as a reference point the current state of emergent shared knowledge and to assist those who are unable to participate frequently and who may otherwise suffer from information overload. Equally, interpretation, elaboration of principal issues and lateral extension of the discussion into new or unforeseen areas are central to the tutorial role. But should summaries be in the nature of a faithful paraphrase of proceedings, or commentary?

Group co-ordination

To limit the debilitating effects of process-loss, certain procedures may be put into place, such as voting facilities — software controlled and mediated or mediated by the tutor; identification of organisational and functional group roles that are performed in rotation by each of the group members; or through allocation of task-specific roles. One of the most effective means of combating process-loss is appointment of a co-ordinator for the group, who thereby enacts certain leadership functions.

Learner training

I have argued that individual skill in the social and information management of CMC interaction is a significant variable in the value of the medium for group interaction. However, pre-course training is frequently restricted to technical aspects of computer-conferencing (access to the system, uploading and downloading, etc.). This can result in novice users facing a steep learning curve as they grapple with the altered social and temporal aspects of CMC interaction in addition to the study component. In order to provide comprehensive preparation for the use of CMC as a mode of group study, a training syllabus might include: technical training; simulation exercises to develop expertise in the social and discourse management of asynchronous exchanges; training in message composition; and training in traditional reading strategies such as skimming and scanning to facilitate offline editing. An additional component of the syllabus might be training in techniques for time-management in view of both the number of different activities concurrently required by CMC interaction, unlike traditional distance study, and socio-emotional pressures that can be caused by participation in 'the virtual classroom' which, during the period of study, never closes.

Conclusion

This chapter describes some of the most prevalent of conditions affecting group interaction across CMC. The next stage of research is to test the validity of the hypotheses made in drawing up the model proposed and to test the validity of the implications of this model; in particular the implication that specification of the CMC tutorial role implies a focus on procedural management rather than direct intervention.

References

Bales, R. (1978) Task roles and social roles in problem-solving groups. In Bradford, L. (ed.) (1978). *Group Development*. La Jolla, CA: University Associates: 152–66.

Brochet, M. (1985) Effective moderation of computer conferences: Notes and suggestions. In Brochet, M. (ed.) (1989): 1–8.

Brochet, M. (ed.) (1989) *Moderating Conferences*. London: X-ON Software Ltd.

Carlson, L. (1986) Effective moderation for computer conferences: hints for moderators. In Brochet, M. (ed.) (1989): 10–13.

Feenburg, A. (1987) Computer conferencing and the Humanities. *Instructional Science* 16(1), 169–86.

Grint, K. (1989) Accounting for failure: participation and non-participation. In Mason, R. and Kaye, A. (eds) (1989) : 189–92.

Handy, C. (1987) *Understanding Organisations*. (3rd edn). Penguin: London.

Harasim, L. (1987) Teaching and learning on-line: Issues in computer-mediated graduate courses. *Canadian Journal for Educational Communication* 16(2), 117–35.

Harasim, L. (ed.) (1990) *Online Education : Perspectives on a New Environment*. New York: Praeger.

Hiltz, S. (1986) The 'Virtual Classroom': Using computer-mediated-communication for university teaching. *Journal of Communication* 36(2), 95–104.

Johansen, R., Vallee, J. and Spangler, K. (1979) *Electronic Meetings: Technical Alternatives and Social Choices*. Reading, MA: Addison-Wesley.

Kaye, A. (ed.) (1992) *Collaborative Learning Through Computer Conferencing*. Berlin: Springer Verlag.

Kerr, E. and Hiltz, S. (1982) *Computer-mediated Communication Systems: Status and Evaluation*. New York: Academic Press.

Kiesler, S. (1992) Talking, teaching and learning in network groups: Lessons from research. In Kaye, A. (ed.) (1992): 147–65.

Kiesler, S., Siegel, J. and McGuire, T. (1984) Social psychological aspects of computer-mediated communication. *American Psychologist* 39(10), 1123–33.

Mason, R. (1989) An evaluation of CoSy on an Open University course. In Mason, R. and Kaye, A. (eds) (1989): 115–145.

Mason, R. and Kaye, A. (eds) (1989) *Mindweave: Communication, Computers and Distance Education*. Oxford: Pergamon.

Rice, R. E. and Associates. (1984) *The New Media: Communication, Research and Technology*. Beverly Hills, CA: Sage.

Siegel, J., Dubrovsky, V., Kiesler, S. and McGuire, T. (1986) Group processes in computer-mediated-communication. *Organisational Behaviour and Human Decision Process* 37, 157–187.

Sorensen, E. and Kaye, A. (1992) Online course design. Paper presented at the conference on Telecommunication in Education and Organisation, Danish Technological Institute, Aarhus, Denmark.

Spitzer, M. (1986) Writing style in computer conferences. *IEEE Transactions on Professional Communications* 29(1), 19–22.

Thomas, R. (1989) The implications of electronic communication for the OU. In Mason, R. and Kaye, A. (eds) (1989): 166–77.

Thorpe, M. (1989) The tutor perspective in computer-mediated-communication. In *Dt200. CITE Report 76*. Milton Keynes: Open University.

Tziner, A., and Eden, D. (1985) Effects of crew composition on crew performance: Does the whole equal the sum of its parts? *Journal of Applied Psychology* 70, 85–93.

10 Inputs and Outputs of Distance Education

RICHARD WEST AND GILLIAN WALSH

Introduction

In this chapter we want to re-examine traditional models of distance learning materials. By revising the concept of 'text' we hope to suggest ways in which input can be made more accessible to learners, and can also help them structure their output.

The School of Education of the University of Manchester has offered modules of its master's degree in TESOL by distance mode since 1988. Initially, these modules were components of free-standing courses run in eastern Europe (O'Brien & West, 1991) but they are now available without restriction on a world-wide basis as part of a master's degree. This chapter should be seen in the context of current developments in the School of Education, which is expanding the range of master's modules offered by distance using the model developed for TESOL. These developments have forced us to analyse and evaluate the approaches we have taken in order to adapt them for other fields of teacher education.

The distance materials that we have offered so far have been predominantly print-based, and most of our discussion here applies to printed materials. However, we now offer certain courses on disk and are moving into CD-ROM, and some of our analysis applies equally to materials offered through such media.

Models of Distance Learning Input and Output

Traditional models

Traditional models of print-based distance-learning materials have various elements, but here we want to focus on what are probably the most common and the most central — the input text and the output tasks. In simple terms, the text is generally a reading text written in continuous prose similar to that in an academic textbook. We might call this 'fully-constructed text'. The tasks are usually backward-looking comprehension checks in or at the end of the text. These tend to test how much of their reading students have understood, and so tend to test knowledge. The format is typically either open-ended *wh*-questions or perhaps multiple-choice items.

Research has shown that students have difficulties in learning from materials built on this model. In a study conducted at the University of Essex into a distance-learning course on the digital computer, Brew (1980: 123) concludes:

> The problem manifests itself in difficulties with sorting out the main points of a text from a supporting explanation (seeing the wood for the trees) and is related to the fact that many students lacked criteria for deciding what was important to learn and also deciding when their study of a text had been adequate.

There seem to be two problems that are relevant:

(1) Processing of the text, i.e. converting input text into student intake and, subsequently, student output available for future application.
(2) Providing immediate feedback to students to indicate whether their processing of the text has been adequate, i.e. whether their output corresponds to the tutor's expectations.

It is evident that conventional academic textbooks do not attempt to address these problems; indeed, they ignore them totally. All too often conventional distance-learning materials also ignore them, except perhaps for an add-on component on study skills or reading strategies. However, the problem is more acute with distance students than it is with residential students studying a textbook in the library, for distance learners tend to be isolated both from fellow students and from tutors.

Alternative models

We will begin by looking at the first of these two problems. In order to process conventional text, a reader has to 'interact' with that text. What is involved in this process of interaction? We may see this as a three-stage process:

reading the writer's constructed input text

↓

de-constructing the input text

↓

re-constructing the input text as the reader's own output text

As language teachers we no longer refer to reading as a passive process, yet all too often it becomes just this. It is very easy for the reader's eyes to glide across the text with very little mental processing: no de-constructing is taking place, no re-constructed text is being formulated by the reader. This approach is especially easy for the hard-pressed distance student at the end of a full-day's work. It is so easily done that the student may not realise what has or (more accurately) what has not taken place.

An obvious solution to this problem is not to present the distance reader with a fully-constructed text as input. If the input text is at least partially de-constructed, the reader has to process it in order to end up with a fully reconstructed text. The process of reading becomes more conscious, the students more aware of their interaction with the text. The more active the processing, the more likely that the learning will be effective and rewarding.

A de-constructed text may take several forms. The most obvious is a text with gaps at certain points, i.e. a cloze text with words, phrases or even whole sentences omitted. The reader is confronted with an incomplete text and has to re-construct it by applying not simply linguistic knowledge (as in a language test) but knowledge of the subject derived from experience, thought or previous reading (including reading of earlier sections of the current text). Another alternative is for the accompanying task to consist of a partially re-constructed version of the input text. Examples might be a set of guided notes, a classification chart, a summary or table. The student then has to process the writer's input text in order to complete the task. The task therefore needs to be presented before the text, to be forward-looking rather than backward-looking. In this way the material provides a solution to the first problem identified by Brew — the task structures the student's reading of the text by providing guidance to gleaning the main points or developing criteria to discern what is important.

Types of Task

To help distance learners with both the problems outlined by Brew we can use forward-looking Self-Assessment Questions (SAQs). The SAQs should, from the above description, promote appropriate re-construction of texts, encouraging learners to interact with the input. The SAQs have a variety of intertwining support functions for text processing (see Figure 10.1).

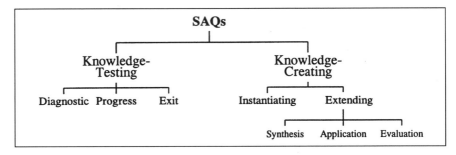

Figure 10.1 Functions of self-assessment questions

From their name it is clear that one of the functions of self-assessment questions is testing. It is useful to distinguish three principal testing functions:

(1) *diagnostic testing* — indicating to the learner what is and is not known about the particular subject at entry to a module, a unit, or a section of a unit;

and/or

(2) *progress testing* — giving the learner indications of what has been learnt so far in the module, unit or section;

and/or

(3) *exit testing* — indicating to the learner what new learning has been achieved from the module, unit or section.

However, in addition to testing functions SAQs may also be used for knowledge-creation. There would seem to be two distinct, but possibly overlapping functions of knowledge-creating questions — those used for *instantiating* purposes and those *extending* existing knowledge.

Instantiating SAQs are used to trigger recall of previous related learning and/or experience. They can be further sub-divided into those that instantiate general, or world knowledge, and those that are more specifically targeted at learners' subject knowledge. Knowledge-*extending* SAQs may be seen to fall into three main categories:

(1) SAQs involving *synthesis* of learning (e.g. analysing, comparing and/or contrasting points from a variety of sources);
(2) SAQs involving *application* of learning (e.g. using new information/ tools to carry out a task);
(3) SAQs involving *evaluation* of learning (i.e. encouraging learners to draw their own conclusions using their own experience in addition to the evidence and tools provided in the materials).

A preliminary examination of 'traditional' non-TESOL distance-learning materials showed that the vast majority of their SAQs were:

• backward looking;
• knowledge-testing.

Figure 10.2 shows that, typically, the few SAQs that had knowledge-creating functions tended to be synthesising, with few in the application category and almost none in the evaluation category.

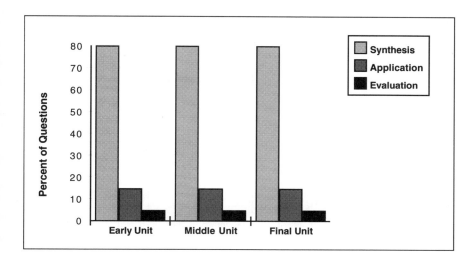

Figure 10.2 SAQ analysis — traditional module

Functions of knowledge-testing and knowledge-creating SAQs are effected through a wide range of task types. It is often the case that, just as a single SAQ may have more than one function, a single task type is used for more than one category of SAQ.

SAQs, then, may be used to help learners with text processing at different stages within a unit and within a whole module of learning. Table 10.1 shows some examples of SAQs used at different points within a unit.

Table 10.1 Examples of SAQs within a unit

SAQ position	SAQ type	Example task types	Help to learners
Introductory (SAQ 0)	Diagnostic (knowledge-testing) and anticipatory (knowledge-creating)*	Y/N, single word/ phrase answers	Show what they already know about the topic, signpost unit contents, stimulate interest, instantiate relevant schema
Early	Synthesising (knowledge-creating)	Identifying, tabulating, ordering, etc	Signal key points, guide re-construction of de-constructed text, help integration of new and previous learning
Middle	Progress (knowledge-testing) and application (knowlege-creating)	Multiple-matching, cognitive cloze, classifying, etc	Signal learning has taken place, emphasise use/relevance of new learning via application tasks
Closing	Progress (knowledge-testing) and evaluation (knowledge-creating)	Experiential — analysing, appraising, concluding	Guide evaluation of new material, formation of informed judgements as to the usefulness of particular approaches, & selection of what is most useful for their purposes
Loop-back	Progress (knowledge-testing) and evaluation (knowledge-creating) *note: this is the second answering of SAQ0*	Y/N, single word/ phrase answers	Re-emphasise & reinforce the learning that has taken place through the unit; encourage construction of own perspective on this learning
Final	Exit (knowledge-testing) and synthesising, application, & evaluation (knowledge-creating)	Assignment-writing tasks: essays, materials + rationale	Stimulate synthesis, application and evaluation of the learning that has taken place through the units in relation to the learner's own teaching context

It would seem desirable that through a distance-learning module the SAQs would move from diagnostic and instantiating in early units to progress, synthesis and application in intermediate units, towards evaluation in the final units. Furthermore, within each individual unit of a module we might also hope to find a similar progression. Thus, as learners progress through a module, we might hope that the proportion of synthesising SAQs would diminish as the proportion of application and evaluation SAQs increases. This idealised distribution is shown in Figure 10.3.

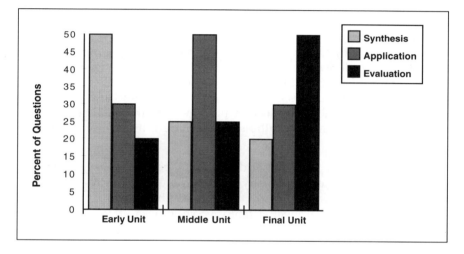

Figure 10.3 SAQ analysis — idealised distribution

The de-construction of the text in conjunction with the SAQs may help overcome Brew's first problem. The answer key to the SAQs may then help with the second problem identified by Brew.

Types of Feedback

Brew's second problem — providing feedback — may be dealt with through the format of the task or SAQ. Providing feedback so that students can decide when and whether their study of the text has been adequate is a further function of SAQs. Such feedback needs to be both frequent and supportive. Frequent feedback suggests that tasks need to be set at regular intervals throughout the text, so that each study session or chunk provides the student with at least one task that may be completed and on which feedback can be given to indicate that learning has been successful. Supportive feedback is facilitated if the task is objective in construction. Open-ended tasks involve learners in deciding whether their answer matches that offered in the answer key. With objective tasks there is no such doubt or insecurity. However, some objective tasks seem to be more effective than others in promoting processing of the input text. Dual-choice tasks — true/false, yes/no — require limited processing in order to make a selection between rather gross or obvious choices. Multiple-choice has similar limitations, encouraging the reader merely to choose one answer from a limited range. It is possible to construct tasks that require more processing yet that remain objective or at least semi-objective. Cloze has already been mentioned. Another fruitful objective format is multiple-matching (see West, 1991), developed recently for computer-based language testing. By offering the reader a far wider range of choice to a longer list of prompts, multiple-matching requires more active and deeper processing of the text that can involve not only selection but also classification, sequencing, defining, etc. Also, unlike multiple choice, it permits several answers to one question.

Objective answers have the added advantage of brevity, so that the distance student can obtain speedy and unambiguous feedback. What is not always clear, however, is how learners can be helped if they get the answer wrong. There are well-established solutions to this problem such as suggesting that the student should read the input text again or should get in touch with the tutor in some way. Neither is a complete solution. It is here than computer-based systems such as Hypertext may offer possibilities that take us beyond those available with print-based materials. We are now investigating these possibilities.

Conclusions

In this chapter we have argued that print-based distance-learning materials are more effective if they break with the traditional approach resembling academic prose. Instead, it has been suggested that materials in which both the text and the task are more structured will enable the course participants to process the input more effectively and the course writers to provide immediate feedback. The two models — traditional and alternative — may be summed up in Table 10.2.

Table 10.2 Models of distance learning materials

	Traditional model	*Alternative model*
Text	fully-constructed	partially de-constructed partially re-constructed
Task	post-reading backward-looking knowledge testing open-ended/subjective	pre-reading/while-reading forward-looking knowledge testing & knowledge creating objective

It should be stressed that materials of the type suggested in the alternative model are seen as a transitional phase. Many distance learners have been away from study for many years and can find academic reading daunting. The alternative proposed here is designed to help ensure that such reading is more structured so that confidence is developed. Immediate and unambiguous feedback provides reassurance that progress is being made in a study situation that is often isolated and lonely. It is only when such confidence has been developed that participants can begin to become fully independent and autonomous learners.

References

Brew, A. (1980) Responses of overseas students to different teaching styles. In *ELT Documents* 109, 115–125.

O'Brien, T. and West, R. (1991) Distance teacher education — From Manchester to Hungary. In *Distance Learning. English Studies* Issue No. 7. London: The British Council: 36–38.

West, R. (1991) Developments in the testing of reading. *World Language English* 1(1), 60–70.

11 Direction and Debate in Distance Materials for Teacher Development

KEITH RICHARDS

Introduction

Because distance-learning (DL) materials lie at the heart of any successful DL course, the pressures on the DL writer/teacher are considerable. Materials production is expensive and time-consuming, and once the materials arrive on students' doorsteps it is too late for second thoughts: 'In a written lesson, your teaching has to be right first time' (Rowntree, 1990: 161).

It is surprising, then, that more research has not been done on the nature of DL materials. Excellent guides exist (for example, Rowntree & Connors, n.d.; Race, 1989; Rowntree, 1990) and much has been written about the work of course teams (e.g. Mason, 1976; Drake, 1979), but the discourse structure of DL materials and student responses to them have not come in for close scrutiny. This is particularly surprising since Holmberg's characterisation (1986: 4) of DL as 'guided didactic conversation', which has been widely accepted, seems to emphasise the importance of discourse (Holmberg, 1991).

One reason for the neglect may be that, where student feedback is unsatisfactory, any investigation is likely to be directed towards pinpointing the source of the problem and making appropriate adjustments as quickly as possible. Problems are therefore regarded as essentially 'local' and there is no incentive to publicise difficulties once they are safely 'in the past'. However, laying bare the process of investigation, however painful, may generate important insights into the nature of DL materials. This chapter is based on such an investigation, the results of which throw interesting light on the conventional advice offered to DL materials writers.

The chapter will begin by providing a brief introduction to a particular component on a DL programme. The results of an investigation into student responses to the course will then be presented. This will be followed by an analysis of certain features of the course in terms of standard advice given to materials writers and in comparison with other courses on the programme. Developing from this, a detailed comparison of this course with a more 'successful' course will be made and key differences in the discourse structure will be identified. The chapter will conclude with suggestions for extending the range of advice currently offered to DL materials writers.

Background

The programme

Linguistic Varieties is one of eight taught components in a DL MSc programme in Teaching English/Teaching English for Specific Purposes offered by the Language Studies Unit of Aston University. The programme was established in 1988 with 25 registered students; it now has around 150. Designed for the experienced English-language teacher with a first degree, it is based on a group methodology and accepts only those applicants who are within reach of a Local Resource Centre established by Aston University. Each group of no more than 15 students is assigned a course tutor who arranges an induction course at the centre, writes a fortnightly newsletter and keeps in contact with students via letter, telephone, fax and e-mail. During the programme, subject specialists also visit the centre.

The programme comprises four 'linguistic' components assessed by examination (Methods of Text and Discourse Analysis, Linguistic Varieties, Descriptions of Modern English and Lexical Studies) and four 'pedagogic' components assessed by assignment (Methodology, Course and Syllabus Design, Materials Analysis and Production and an option) as well as a dissertation. There are four taught phases, each lasting roughly four months and each containing two components. Relevant component files are despatched to students before the start of each phase and prior to the start of the course students receive a *Course Guide*, dealing with administrative matters, and a *Study Companion*. The latter contains advice on academic study and writing as well as introductions to all courses with lists of key texts (annotated) and further reading for each unit.

The course

Linguistic Varieties (LV) appears in the second phase with Course and Syllabus Design, following Methods of Text and Discourse Analysis and Methodology. It is designed to introduce students to the ways in which spoken interaction and relevant language varieties are studied and analysed, and to this end it draws on three overlapping areas: sociolinguistics, the ethnography of communication and ethnomethodology. Like all components except options, the LV file consists of ten units, each divided into three coloured sections: discussion, exercises and resources. This arrangement has received very positive feedback and is now standard.

While other components have had a smooth passage, this particular course has been rewritten twice. The first writer left shortly after completing the original version called 'Linguistic Features of Varieties of ESP' and it was decided that the component should be renamed and rewritten. A course team was established and produced a new course that was popular with students but that staff considered academically undemanding. A new member of staff was appointed and asked to rewrite the course completely over two years. It is this final version that is the subject of this study.

The writer's brief

Although new to DL, the writer was an experienced teacher of English for Specific Purposes with an excellent track record in his chosen field. He has also published papers in international journals and produced teacher development materials. He was happy about writing the course and was able to combine this with two years of teaching an in-house course covering the same ground. The prospects for a successful course therefore seemed excellent.

I was involved in briefing the writer and had responsibility for approving the course. We discussed at length the drawbacks of previous versions and the need for a suitably academic but nevertheless practical orientation, and before beginning to write, he outlined in detail what his objectives were and how he planned to achieve them. His perspective, which involved offering students as much freedom as possible in their choice of topics, was not entirely in line with other components but seemed exactly right for this particular course. A draft of the first unit was seen and approved by three members of staff and feedback was provided on subsequent units, but the course did not receive a full trial.

Feedback

Feedback on the distance learning programme takes a number of forms:

- standard evaluation forms in each component file;
- a standard evaluation form at the end of the programme;
- specific evaluation forms covering, e.g. groups, videos;
- anonymous feedback from centres (sometimes collated by an individual student) to the course tutor;
- anonymous comments written at feedback sessions held by course tutors;
- informal comments to tutors.

Informal feedback suggested very early on that students were finding this course very difficult and were unhappy with the materials, an impression that was confirmed at formal feedback sessions and on the component feedback forms. These forms work on the basis of three categories, 'less than satisfactory', 'satisfactory' and 'more than satisfactory', and it is extremely rare to find ticks in the first category. The feedback on LV was disturbing, particularly in the light of the writer's experience and popularity as a teacher and in view of our own assessment of the materials. It therefore became important not just to make changes to the course but to find out as much as possible about where its weaknesses lay.

Student Responses

Student responses were collected by three means:

- standard evaluation forms;
- unstructured interviews;
- detailed written feedback on selected extracts.

Together, these provided a useful starting point for an analysis of the component itself.

Standard evaluation forms

The first step in establishing the nature of the problem was to check the course evaluation forms. While some students noted the 'richness of the topics covered in the component', this had to be set against a more general impression summed up by one student as follows:

> I read and re-read these materials over a period of weeks. I found them virtually impossible to understand! Many others reported the same experience.

Interviews

In order to probe this further, individual interviews were arranged with seven members of one of the overseas groups. These interviews, which were taped, were unstructured and lasted between 5 and 20 minutes. They were useful not least because there was considerable uniformity in the responses. Three of the respondents emphasised the enjoyment they had derived from the course and all mentioned the broadness of the area — one described his experience as like 'stepping into a vast wilderness'. Most suggested that a map or outline would have been a great help and many referred to an impression of disjointedness, which may account for difficulties many found in getting into the course. The following extract from one of the interviewees could be taken to speak for them all:

> It was very interesting and enjoyable. . . . It was very hard to get into. . . . A lot of the text was very hard to follow. It seemed very disjointed. It wasn't until the very end of the course that I had a grip on what was going on, what the content was. Then going back at the end of the course, the units made sense.

Interviews did not provide the best means of eliciting specific comments on the text itself; to do this it was necessary to invite written comments on extracts from the course.

Detailed comments on extracts

Two extracts (seven pages in all) from the first unit of the course were sent to twenty students in two of the groups. An accompanying letter explained that many students had found the component difficult to read and invited respondents to mark the extracts, indicating and commenting on any problems that they encountered. Eight students replied and all but one of them provided detailed comments. The exception highlighted words that he considered could have been included in a glossary, and this threw useful light on some of the comments made by others. Of the remaining seven, one student was entirely positive about the extract and the course.

Negative comments could be grouped under three headings:

Interruptions

Nearly all of the respondents complained that the flow of the argument was constantly interrupted and one student summed up the problem as follows: 'Assuming [students] are "into the swing" of study it is unhelpful to be told to stop (it is after all hard enough to start).' The following were mentioned:

- the need to have relevant articles to hand;
- requests to read articles;
- exercises;
- requests to spend time thinking;
- excessive use of quotation marks, bold face type, parentheses and italics for emphasis, references, examples, etc.;
- a less clear distinction between discussion and resources sections than on other components.

Lack of clear reference

Half the respondents made comments that can be grouped under this general heading. The following specific examples were offered:

- unclear anaphoric reference ('these terms', etc.);
- misleading signalling and enumeration ('Secondly's just didn't appear.');
- vague statements.

Lack of adequate explanation

This featured in all but one of the responses and was variously described. The following points were mentioned specifically:

- a large number of references and technical terms;
- many technical terms not explained;
- mention of names without reference to what they represent;
- unwarranted assumptions about reader's knowledge;
- purpose of questions/tasks not made clear.

This feedback clearly indicated the need for further investigation, and from a practical point of view there were advantages in considering these comments in the light of standard advice on DL materials writing.

Listening to Advice

One immediate problem in using standard sources of advice, which seem to be written predominantly with undergraduate courses in mind, is that the design of this programme is fundamentally different from that of such courses. From the outset, the aim was to ensure that this Master's course could be distinguished from them. Emphasis is therefore placed on 'opening up' academic territory to students by treating printed materials as a point of departure. Once the subject has been introduced, students can select from the reading lists in the *Study Companion* in order to extend their enquiries in directions that they find interesting.

The best way of representing the difference between this and conventional approaches is to say that while the general advice is to think of the materials as a 'tutorial-in-print' (Rowntree, 1990), here they represent a lecture (discussion section) followed by tasks (exercises section) and personal investigation (resources section and *Study Companion*). Some exercises are integrated into the text but not as tightly or as frequently as in conventional materials. There is also much less variation in terms of format and hardly any use of visual materials. The result may be visually 'dry' but it is meant to be academically 'juicy'. Obviously, the validity of this is open to question at a general level, but the feedback from students has been very positive: there is almost universal support for the three-part structure and the ideas behind it. It should also be noted that the question-and-answer nature of a tutorial is also an important feature of the lecture and an *essential* feature of DL materials.

Criticisms from students in the 'interruptions' category were obviously keenly felt, so it was important to explore this aspect of the text. A comparison was therefore made between this course and another in the programme in order to highlight differences. Since students had been sent extracts from the first unit, this was chosen as the focus for analysis and compared with the equivalent unit from Methods of Text and Discourse Analysis (TDA). This course immediately precedes LV but is examined at the same time and is similar in terms of content, as the titles of the opening units indicate: 'Language and Context' (LV), 'Context, Text and Discourse' (TDA). More importantly, it is a very popular course, attracting universally positive feedback that often includes comments on the clarity of its presentation and exposition.

It was therefore very surprising to find that expected differences between the courses did not emerge. In view of students' observations on the number of references and the amount of emphasis, it was reasonable to assume that a straightforward count would show up significant differences between the two courses. The number of writers mentioned and the instances of emphasis (words or phrases appearing in bold print, capitals, italics or inverted commas, excluding quotations or sample texts for illustration) were therefore calculated and expressed as a percentage of the total number of sentences in the unit (see Table 11.1).

Table 11.1 Incidence of emphasis and references expressed as a percentage of the total number of sentences

	LV(%)	TDA(%)
Emphasis	35.9	38.5
References	11.8	17.3
Total	47.7	55.8

The situation was the reverse of what student comments indicated. However, a simple count will not reflect the distribution of such features throughout the unit. It may be, for example, that such 'interruptions' are scattered throughout LV but more strategically grouped in the TDA unit. An analysis of the distribution in paragraphs provided a useful picture (see Table 11.2).

Table 11.2 Distribution of emphasis and references in paragraphs

	LV(%)	TDA(%)
Paras with emphasis only	20.0	32.5
Paras with references only	16.8	15.0
Paras with both	50.5	35.0
Paras with neither	12.6	17.5

Although this pointed in the expected direction and the number of paragraphs containing both emphasis and references in LV is interesting, it does not seem to provide strong support for criticisms made by the students. The figures would certainly not provide a convincing case for asking a materials writer to reduce the amount of emphasis and the number of references in a particular unit. It was fairly clear from this analysis that students' *perceptions* of the amount of 'interruption' had been influenced by their reading of the text as a whole rather than by the number of times interruptions occurred and that the problem lay at a deeper, discoursal level. Evidently, advice on varying style and using exercises that is usually given to materials writers could not be used to respond to this particular problem.

It was possible, of course, that the writing itself was 'dense' (more than one respondent had used this expression) and that 'interruptions' acted as a last straw. Advice on DL materials writing emphasises the importance of a 'conversational style' and 'plain writing'. The following represent a summary of key points presented in three standard sources (Rowntree & Connors, n.d.; Race, 1989; Rowntree, 1990):

Conversational style

- Use personal pronouns and contractions.
- Use rhetorical questions.
- Maintain a light touch and don't ignore the human angle.

Plain writing

- Use short, familiar words and phrases.
- Keep sentences short (allowing for variety).
- Use strong, active vocabulary.
- Take care with specialist vocabulary.

Since it is hard to determine what constitutes a 'light touch' and the 'human angle', these had to be ignored, and specialist vocabulary overlapped too closely with emphasis to make further investigation of it worthwhile. The same applied to rhetorical questions, which hardly featured in any of the courses in the programme. However, all other elements could be checked: personal pronouns were counted, the proportion of active sentences was established and sentence and word length were also checked. Finally, the readability formulas suggested in the three sources (Flesch and Fog) were applied. The first unit was again used for the purposes of comparison, but this time all courses in the programme were involved.

In terms of the LV course, a comparison of personal pronouns (Table 11.3) was no more revealing than the check on references and emphasis. Since standard advice links the use of personal pronouns to involvement and an 'informal' style, first and second person subject pronouns were selected and 'let us' or its contraction was added in case this made a significant difference. The result, expressed in terms that might be used to advise a novice writer, is that about one in three sentences should contain one of these items — a crude formulation but still uncomfortably prescriptive. Although some of the courses fall way outside this general guideline (Methodology includes double the number, while Lexical Studies manages barely one-sixth), LV is close enough for comfort.

Table 11.3 Personal pronouns in first units expressed as percentage of total number of sentences

	I	We	You	Let's	All
Methodology	—	40.8	28.2	01.0	70.0
TDA	08.3	19.9	04.5	00.6	33.3
Course & Syll.	03.9	36.4	03.9	02.6	46.8
Materials A&P	05.4	01.8	09.4	01.8	18.4
Management ELT	—	08.6	12.3	—	20.9
Classroom Res.	00.7	08.3	44.1	—	53.1
Self-Access/DL	—	09.6	25.6	—	35.2
Teacher Prep.	19.4	04.5	20.1	01.5	45.5
Business Eng.	—	22.1	07.4	02.9	32.4
Lexical Studies	—	03.8	—	01.3	05.1
Desc. Modern Eng.	13.8	02.2	17.4	—	33.4
LV	08.2	06.6	12.6	00.8	28.2
Mean	05.0	13.7	15.5	01.0	35.2

Extending the analysis to readability (Table 11.4) simply confirms the pattern, although this analysis was generated by the computer's own 'grammar check' and must therefore be regarded as a *very* rough guide. The first LV unit is much longer than any of the others (a factor not mentioned in the feedback), but in terms of readability it is again close to the norm on all the measures. Although this norm is by no means standard, feedback over five years indicates that it represents what students on this course like and indeed expect. The 17-word 'standard' sentence used by the Flesch index, for example, is about three-quarters the length of the 'standard' sentence here, but this may simply be a reflection of the programme's academic orientation. Similarly, while 12 on the Fog Index has been proposed as a useful maximum (Rowntree, 1990), none of the courses here falls below 13 and many of them have been praised for their clarity. It may be true that 'The only people who tend to be insulted by simple language in learning material seem to be academics' (Race, 1989: 76), but this does not undermine the value of more complex expression when this is appropriate and when the audience — in our case teachers working at Master's level — are able to appreciate and respond to it. There is also evidence that texts simplified using standard readability formulas are in fact no easier to read than their 'denser' originals (Olsen & Johnson, 1989), though this needs to be set against research that indicates that such formulas have proved useful in DL materials analysis (Macdonald-Ross, 1979).

Table 11.4 Readability of DL courses (computer-generated)

	Words	Char. ters	Paras	Sent- ences	Sents per para	Wds per sent	Chars per word	Flesch Pass sents	Flesch read. ease	Gun. grade level	Flesch -Kinc.	Fog Ind.
Methodology	2295	13667	34	103	3	22	4	28	49.7	13.0	11.2	14.1
Text & Disc.	4200	25695	40	156	3	26	4	24	45.7	13.6	12.5	15.2
Course & Syll.	2031	12039	26	77	2	26	4	27	51.0	12.6	11.5	14.7
Materials A&P	4515	27996	56	223	3	20	4	26	44.0	13.8	11.7	14.2
Man. ELT	2069	13329	22	81	3	25	5	56	30.3	15.9	15.0	17.6
Class Research	3293	19616	36	145	4	22	4	25	54.5	11.6	10.5	13.1
Self Access/DL	3338	20041	33	156	4	21	4	25	47.6	13.3	11.2	13.7
Teacher Prep.	2797	16717	32	134	4	20	4	18	51.3	12.5	10.8	13.4
Business	1588	10394	22	68	3	23	5	33	31.6	15.7	14.3	17.4
Lexical Studies	4309	28515	32	160	5	26	5	33	26.5	17.0	15.0	17.6
Desc. Mod. Eng.	3428	21048	25	138	5	24	4	26	44.3	13.8	12.5	14.6
Ling. Var.	7573	47549	95	365	3	20	5	14	42.6	14.1	11.9	14.5
MEAN	3453	21384	38	150	3.5	23	4.3	28	43.3	13.9	12.3	15.0

In terms of advice on writing, the only area where LV stands out is in the number of passive sentences it contains. The figure for this was generated by a computer programme that had no accompanying explanation, so there is the possibility of some distortion. A grammar check using the system suggests that the count is based on verb groups and this means that sentences that are not essentially passive may be counted as such. For example, in the sentence beginning 'Similarly...' in the previous paragraph, only the subordinate clause is in the passive: 'while 12 on the Fog Index <u>has been proposed</u>. . . none of the courses here fall. . .' (words underlined are those highlighted in the check). Similarly, the penultimate sentence contains a verb group in the passive but in a defining relative clause which is part of the subject ('The only people who tend <u>to be insulted</u>. . . seem to be. . .'). Even bearing this in mind, the figure for passive sentences in LV is remarkably low. In this, at least, it seems to be following standard advice more closely than any of the other courses.

The consequences of all this for advice on materials writing are slightly disturbing. It would seem that student impressions provide an inadequate basis for generalisation and that meeting the criteria laid down for effective writing is no guarantee of success. It is extremely difficult, of course, to lay down rules for good writing, and the writers referred to here (e.g. Rowntree, 1990) can hardly be blamed for any failings in this course. I would certainly not wish to argue that their advice is unsound, but on the basis of the analysis so far it is hard to avoid the conclusion that it is incomplete. In purely practical terms, there is no evidence here that the writing in the LV file fails to meet adequate criteria for DL materials writing, and pointing the writer in the direction of standard sources of advice would not be likely to help much. In fact, the materials were written in the light of such advice in so far as it applied to the DL programme. It was therefore necessary to extend the scope of the investigation to the discourse structure of the units — something that has not been addressed in DL literature.

Discourse and Debate

Sentences are usually regarded as 'the largest clearly definable' linguistic entities, 'grammatical or ungrammatical, and meaningful or meaningless, depending upon whether they are constructed in accordance with the appropriate linguistic rules' (Sanford & Garrod, 1981: 4–5). It is hard to apply equivalent descriptive terms to longer stretches of text. Numerous models and methods have been proposed for analysing discourse, and our understanding of discourse structure has deepened considerably as a result, but definitive rules remain as elusive as ever. What follows, therefore, represents at best a tentative effort to draw on a vast and varied body of research in order to throw some light on DL materials writing.

A clue to one line of enquiry emerged, perhaps fortuitously, in the first of the interviews with students, which immediately followed a more general discussion related to a dissertation topic:

> We've just talked about general and specific and I felt I was getting a lot of specifics and I had no picture of the general. I just couldn't piece it together.

The relationship between general and specific in the development of discourse is one of a cluster of concepts that relate information structure to text and sentence organisation. Put very crudely, at the heart of this is the idea that text is 'about' something. This 'something' can be described as the 'Theme'. Although the precise definition of the term is still a matter of some debate (Fries & Francis, 1992), I shall use Halliday's version: the Theme is the 'point of departure of the message' (1985: 38) or a 'peg on which the message is hung' (1970: 161). The Theme always appears first in a clause and what lies outside the Theme (the rest of the clause) is described as the Rheme. At paragraph level, it is also possible to regard the 'topic sentence' as the Theme (Halliday, 1985: 56).

Closely connected with this distinction is that between 'Given' and 'New' information. Given information is that which is recoverable, either because it has been previously mentioned or because it is present in a shared environment or as part of assumed mutual knowledge. New information is not recoverable. In writing, as Bloor & Bloor point out (1992: 34), a major problem is 'how to carry the reader along with the writer's assumptions about what is and what is not shared information in the absence of the possibility of negotiation of meaning such as is available to participants in face to face interaction'. This formulation is uncannily close to the way in which the challenge of distance learning itself has been expressed.

The solution depends on how 'old' information is related to what is being introduced for the first time. It helps if attention can be drawn to 'mutual' knowledge as a point of departure, which means that the Given should appear in the Theme position at the beginning of the clause. New information can then be introduced at the end, since 'other things being equal, reading is easier when the New information is presented in the Rheme position' (Bloor & Bloor, 1992: 35). The writer can then develop the text through the choice of Theme. For example, the Theme of one sentence might be the Rheme of the previous one (as in sentence 2 below), or it could be the Theme from an earlier sentence (as in sentence 3 below), especially if this happens to be the main topic of the paragraph:

(1)   I've just seen <u>Harry</u>.
(2)   <u>He</u> was wearing his new uniform.
(3)   <u>He</u> didn't look very happy.

This is a very basic statement of the Theme/Rheme relationship, which does not reflect either its complexity or its subtlety. However, it is possible to enrich the description by adding further observations related to it:

(1)   Links between sentences are obviously important (for a full discussion see Halliday & Hasan, 1976) and need to be clear. If the second sentence in the example above had read 'He was with Jim' the referent of 'He' at the beginning of the third sentence would have been unclear.
(2)   Danes (1974: 121, quoted in Bloor & Bloor 1992) refers to a 'double theme' or 'double rheme', each part of which can then be developed, as in the following example: 'ESP is often divided into EAP and EOP.

EAP is concerned with English that is used in educational settings such as schools, colleges and universities. EOP, however, focuses on occupational English, often in business or the professions.'

(3) The Theme/Rheme relationship can be extended to paragraph organisation. Fries & Francis, for example, note that 'most of the examples of analysed paragraphs we have seen in systemic descriptions fit the type "generalisation (= Theme) followed by specifics (= Rheme)"' (1992: 49). This corresponds to the findings of writers from different analytic traditions. It is similar, for example, to the 'general → specific' relationship that comes at the top of Van Dijk's list for 'normal ordering' in text (1977: 106) and to Hoey's (1983) 'preview-detail' characterisation.

In this general description, I have tried to introduce what I believe is a useful tool for textual analysis. What really matters in the context of distance learning, however, is whether this can be expressed in terms of straightforward guidelines that could supplement existing advice. I believe it can, and with relatively little modification. First, the focus should be on the sentence and the paragraph. For very good reasons, work in this area has focused on the clause, but reference to this might confuse rather than enlighten some DL writers. Secondly, the 'beginning' and 'end' of sentences should be used as a point of reference and should be interpreted rather loosely. This produces the following set of rough and ready 'guidelines':

(1) It is better to move from general to specific. Bear this in mind when organising paragraphs.
(2) Sentences should begin with something *Given*, i.e. something that the reader already knows, either because it is part of his/her background knowledge or because it has already been introduced in the text.
(3) *New* information should be introduced after this.
(4) In terms of Given-New information, the following sequence of patterns is useful:
   A (GIVEN) → B (NEW)
   B (GIVEN) → C (NEW)
   B (GIVEN) → D (NEW)
(5) The following refinement is also possible:
   A (GIVEN) → B + C (NEW)
   B (GIVEN) → D (NEW)
   C (GIVEN) → E (NEW)
(6) Make sure that all references to earlier items ('this', 'it', 'she' etc.) are clear.

Writers should treat these as crude descriptive tools or guidelines for analysis rather than as rules: effective DL writing should not be attempted in a straitjacket. Similarly, these 'guidelines' should not be used as a means of judging DL writing, but where problems arise they can be used as diagnostic tools. Their effectiveness in this role can be illustrated by applying them to related extracts in the LV and TDA courses.

In order to make the selection of extracts as fair as possible, it was based on the LV extracts sent out to students. The paragraph chosen was the first of two that were the target of a number of specific comments from students. Fortunately, the choice of an equivalent section from TDA was very straightforward: where the LV section ('The Speech Event Model') begins with 'Despite a long standing awareness of links between language and culture, evident in the ethnography of Franz Boas, Edward Sapir, Benjamin Whorf and, on this side of the Atlantic, Bronislaw Malinowski...' the TDA section ('Competence & Performance vs Communicative Competence') ends with 'Hymes was not saying anything new, since anthropological linguists (Sapir, Whorf, Boas in America, Firth and Malinowski in Britain)...'. All that remained was to select a paragraph of suitable length.

Here, then, is an analysis of the TDA extract (original emphasis removed, concluding quotation omitted). The analysis is necessarily crude since I have worked at the sentence level, but the pattern of the text emerges clearly (G=Given; N=New; key items of 'information' are indicated by lower case letters and are related to the preceding underlined item):

> The great Swiss linguist, Ferdinand de Saussure [Ga], made a distinction between what he called langue [Nb] and parole [Nc]. Although these terms [Gb+c] are sometimes translated as 'language' and 'speech' (Nd), it is more usual, and probably less confusing to use the original French terms [Ne], bearing in mind that they are technical terms [Nf] and that in their normal use in French they do not carry the precise meaning of de Saussure's usage [Ng]. Roughly, langue [Gb] is the language system, the linguistic heritage of the community [Nh], and parole [Gc] is the actual realisation of that system in practice [Ni]. Chomsky [Gx] takes up this distinction with some modification and difference of emphasis in his use of the terms competence [Nj] and performance [Nk]. Competence [Gj] he defines as 'the speaker-hearer's knowledge of his language' [Nl] and performance [Gk] as 'the actual use of language in concrete situations' [Nm]. Chomsky [Gx] proposes only to investigate competence since, as he says,
>
> (*Words*: 144)

This extract illustrates many of the points mentioned. The relationship between Given-New and Theme-Rheme is obvious: prior Rhemes become a subsequent Theme (Nb+Nc → Gb+c), in two cases (b,c and j,k) there are 'double themes/rhemes', and there is repetition of a Theme (x). In addition, the text moves from general to specific in the sense that it begins with a general distinction which is followed by comment, characterisation and modification.

The extract from LV is less easy to analyse, even allowing for the fact that the sentence rather than the clause is the basis for analysis:

A second initial question [Ga] to consider is: what do we mean by 'structures of linguistic life' [Nb]? I have already discussed the answer in general terms of patterns [Gb] and constraints (or 'rules') [Gc]. Taking this [Gb+c] further, you would look for these patterns at different communicative levels: societal (institutional), group and individual [Nd] (cf Saville-Troike 1989:13). To illustrate [this] [Gd], let us consider not words but the spaces between and around them, where silence speaks as loud, sometimes louder [Ne]. Speech [Gf] is one form of communicative behaviour [Ng] and ethnographers of speaking use the term to stand for other modes, including of course writing, and silence [Nh]. The leading sociolinguistic questions [Ni] of what can be said, where, when, by whom, to whom, how and in what circumstances [Nb] will also therefore be put in the negative: who may not speak about what and in what situations [Nc]?

(*Words*: 138)

The extract begins with a 'second initial question' that is assumed to be Given. However, the 'first initial question' occurs, if at all, two paragraphs back as 'Ask yourself first, what is context in this approach?' The Given is not easily recoverable. The same applies to the previous discussion [Gb+c], which is very hard to track down. This sentence is followed, however, by two clear Rheme-Theme links (b+c, d), after which the pattern breaks down. It is particularly confusing to find a reference to silence in the Rheme position, immediately followed by 'Speech' in the Theme position. The relevance of the New information that follows (g and h) is therefore easy to relate to speech but not to preceding sentences. The sentence following this is confusing because it begins with New information (it is not recoverable from what has so far appeared and, for a newcomer to the field, cannot be assumed knowledge) and hence falls under what Bloor & Bloor (1992: 37) call 'the problem of the Brand New Theme'. In addition, it moves on to New information (b,c) that is actually linked to earlier Given information in the second sentence — though for someone unfamiliar with the area the link may remain hidden.

There are various ways in which this paragraph might be changed, but the 'Brand New Theme' problem must be avoided and the link between Gb+c and Nb+c needs to be established. This can be achieved with relatively little alteration to the text. In the following passage, I have made the necessary changes and added (unchanged) the paragraph that followed this one in the unit:

> What do we mean by 'structures of linguistic life'? The answer will involve a consideration of patterns (what can be said, where, when, by whom, to whom, how, and in what circumstances) and constraints (who may not speak about what and in what circumstances). Taking this further, you would look for these patterns at different levels: societal (institutional), group and individual. To illustrate this, let us consider not words but the spaces between and around them, where silence speaks as loud, sometimes louder. In that theoretically least 'exotic' of social settings, the family, you can probably think of some ways in which silence patterns on the different dimensions. Certain rituals (the 9 O'Clock News) or taboos ('We don't talk to Auntie Rita') exert an influence; certain norms apply to some groups in the family ('children should be seen and not heard', 'go to your room'); and at an individual level silence will mark certain roles (listener in conversation), statuses (not interrupting Great Aunt Vi), attitudes (sulking, being 'stuck up', being 'cool') or talk-in-the-head (prayer, fantasy) (see Saville-Troike & Tannen, 1985).

By following the guidelines more closely and bearing in mind the importance of a question-and-answer approach, it is possible to produce the following:

> What do we mean by 'structures of linguistic life'? They comprise communicative patterns and constraints operating at different levels. So questions of what can be said or not said, where, when, by whom, to whom and in what circumstances can be answered at different levels: societal (institutional), group and individual. To illustrate this, let's focus on the family and consider patterns of silence operating at different levels there. In the family as a whole, rituals or taboos will determine when silence is appropriate: 'The 9 O'Clock News is on', 'We don't talk to Auntie Rita'. Some groups in the family will have certain norms which apply to them: 'Children should be seen and not heard', 'Go to your room'. At an individual level, silence will mark certain roles (listener in conversation), statuses (not interrupting Great Aunt Vi), attitudes (sulking, being 'stuck up', being 'cool') or talk-in-the-head (prayer, fantasy). For further discussion, see Saville-Troike & Tannen (1985).

Here the question has been simply stated and immediately answered, with some elaboration and extended exemplification, making use of the Theme/Rheme links outlined earlier. It is not necessarily a 'better' version, but it is more accessible.

Conclusion

The purpose of this chapter has been to show how investigation into problematic materials can be rewarding. As a result of one such investigation, it has been possible to draw up a list of guidelines that supplement current advice on materials writing. If these guidelines prove to be of use to DL writers, either when they first approach their task or in the editing stage, this investigation will have been worthwhile. However, its conclusions need to be set in the context of more fundamental concerns.

There is no doubt that students do not find this course an easy one and an analysis of its discourse structure indicates why the LV 'debate' as presented here is hard to follow. But this does not mean that it is a *bad* course. Staff reaction to it has been very positive and students, when they have completed the course, come to appreciate the riches it has to offer. It is not an easy course because it was never meant to be. The writer begins an introduction to it as follows:

> Linguistic Varieties can seem like a Los Angeles of a course on first acquaintance: a sociolinguistic sprawl, no real downtown and lots of freeways with no apparent pattern to them. I like Los Angeles and I like the course, they make sense to me, but I am happy to acknowledge that there are flaws in both.

I happen to share his views, and I think it is important that, while we need to recognise the importance of a clear style and 'lightness of touch', we also need to remember that there are alternative ways of approaching materials writing, that the 'standard' advice is simply that — there should be no prescription. In a sense this course has no direction and that *is* its direction. As to its value, I leave the last word to one of the students who followed it:

> It breathed and it was alive and there was something very human about it.

Acknowledgements

I should like to thank the students from the Japan and UK groups for their valuable and detailed feedback on the LV course. I should also like to thank my colleagues Julian Edge and Alison Birch for their helpful comments and suggestions on the first draft of this paper.

References

Bloor, M. and Bloor T. (1992) Given and New information in the thematic organization of text: An application to the teaching of academic writing. In Noèl, D. (ed.) (1992): 33–43.

Daneš, F. (1974) Functional sentence perspective and the organization of the text. In Daneš, F. (ed.) (1974) *Papers on Functional Sentence Perspective*. The Hague: Mouton: 106–128.

Drake, M. (1979) The curse of the course team. *Teaching at a Distance* 16, 50–53.

Fries, P. and Francis, G. (1992) Exploring Theme: problems for research. In Noèl, D. (ed.) (1992): 45–59.

Halliday, M. (1970) Language structure and language function. In Lyons, J. (ed.) (1970) *New Horizons in Linguistics*. Harmondsworth: Penguin: 140–164.

Halliday, M. (1985) *An Introduction to Functional Grammar*. London: Arnold.

Halliday, M. and Hasan, R. (1976) *Cohesion in English*. London: Longman.

Hoey, M. (1983) *On the Surface of Discourse*. London: George Allen & Unwin.

Holmberg, B. (1986) *Growth and Structure of Distance Education*. London: Croom Helm.

Holmberg, B. (1991) Testable theory based on discourse and empathy. *Open Learning* 6 (2), 44–46.

Macdonald-Ross, M. (1979) Language in texts: A review of research relevant to the design of curricular materials. In Schulman, L. (ed.) (1979). *Review of Research in Education* 6. Itasca, IL: Peacock: 229–275.

Mason, J. (1976) Life inside the course team. *Teaching at a Distance* 5, 27–33.

Noèl, D. (ed.) (1992) *Occasional Papers in Systemic Linguistics* Volume 6. Nottingham: Nottingham English Language and Linguistics Research Group.

Olsen, L. and Johnson, R. (1989) Towards a better measure of readability: explanation of empirical performance results. *Word* 40, 223–34.

Race, P. (1989) *The Open Learning Handbook: Selecting, Designing and Supporting Open Learning Materials*. London: Kogan Page.

Rowntree, D. (1990) *Teaching Through Self-instruction* (rev. edn). London: Kogan Page.

Rowntree, D. and Connors, B. (n.d.) *How to Develop Self-Instructional Teaching: a Self-instructional Guide to the Writing of Self-instructional Materials*. Milton Keynes: Open University.

Sanford, A. and Garrod, S. (1981) *Understanding Written Language*. Chichester: Wiley.

Van Dijk, T. (1977) *Text and Context*. London: Longman.

12 Monitoring the Effectiveness of Distance Learning as a Means of Partially Delivering Teacher Education

RAY PARKER AND TIM GRAHAM

Introduction

A major contention of this chapter is that in initial teacher education in the area of intensive TESOL courses, a distance-learning (DL) component can act as a significant platform for foundation work upon which it is then possible to build during a direct contact phase. It is a generalisation, though no doubt true, to say that most people enrolling on initial TESOL programmes do so with only a relatively slender grasp of their native language in any objective sense. Intuitive users of a language are not necessarily effective exemplifiers of it. In short, their language awareness will tend to be limited. It thus has to be a primary objective of course providers to substantially raise this awareness so that qualifying teachers come to have an active knowledge of the language system and its parts. An effectively organised programme of DL can play a major role in starting off what will hopefully be a continuing process of growing linguistic objectivity in teachers.

At Sheffield Hallam University, the TESOL Centre endeavours to initiate such a process by preparing students through a three-month DL programme that precedes a four-week full-time study block and a subsequent four-week DL assignment. The syllabuses for the DL component are discussed by Haworth and Parker (Chapter 6); in broad terms they are grouped into core units covering aspects of the sound system of English, language awareness and general background reading. A total of approximately 180 hours of directed study is delivered in DL mode. We have found that the advantage of such an approach is that students arrive for the full-time phase of the course well primed in these key areas and already possessing an awareness of general principles and terminology specific to the field.

As DL forms such a major part of the basic input of the course, the Centre is particularly concerned to ensure its objectives are being met. Beliefs such as those outlined above clearly need evaluation and confirmation or modification and it is this area of evaluation that we will present in the paper.

Evaluation of the quality of experience for distance learners on our courses has taken many forms over the past few years and has led to both minor and radical modification of materials and to recommissioning materials that needed more than modification, decommissioning materials where experience showed that DL was not an effective vehicle for delivery and commissioning new materials where gaps were found.

Almost all of the evaluation has been learner-centred and has focused on the collection and consideration of feedback from the users of the materials themselves. In this way, the Centre has attempted to generate an interactive feedback model and avoided having a tutor-led approach alone.

The mass of information gathered in this way falls into four categories depending on the timing of the feedback exercise.

These categories are as follows:

(1) Feedback from DL users during and throughout the DL phase via a response pro-forma relating to each module of study that has been submitted and assessed and returned to the student. Students have the opportunity here to react on an incremental basis to the comments of assessing tutors and to ask for clarification or further information. Although the return of the pro-formas is optional, most students do return them.

(2) Feedback given at a point in time during the DL phase via a questionnaire that seeks to define the quality of the experience.

(3) Feedback after the DL phase of the course is complete via a questionnaire that seeks to define the quality of the experience.

(4) Feedback after the direct contact phase has been completed via a questionnaire that seeks to define the value of the DL phase within the structure of the course as a whole.

Figure 12.1 summarises the measures used on different courses for experimental purposes, the particular foci of experimentation being:

- the value of response pro-formas;
- the relative utility of questionnaires used during rather than on completion of the distance learning phase.

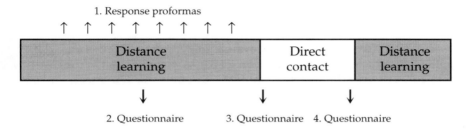

Figure 12.1 Evaluation techniques employed

By synthesizing the results of such quality control and feedback mechanisms we can begin to form some tentative conclusions regarding the role and value of a DL component in initial teacher education for TESOL. Just as important for the present discussion, we may be able to assess the contribution of specific feedback mechanisms and any effects relating to the timing of these mechanisms. A further description of the evaluative techniques employed follows.

Response Pro-formas

The first category referred to, the response pro-formas, was originally piloted as an experimental research study whereby half a Certificate in TESOL cohort was provided with feedback response slips (Appendix 12.1) with the other half continuing with what had until then been the normal pattern: tutor-led feedback only. In a subsequent review of the DL phase during the direct contact phase, those course members who had received the feedback response slips expressed feelings of greater involvement in the course and said they had found the dual feedback process beneficial to DL study. The experimental nature of the process was continued with the following cohort and the same general pattern emerged. Thereafter all course members on each cohort were provided with feedback response slips. Data gathered since this change and indicating user response to feedback is set out in Table 12.1.

Table 12.1 Course member response to feedback during distance learning phase ($n = 133$)

Positive%	Mixed%	Negative%
88.7	8.3	3

Questionnaires

The next two categories of evaluation employed the same data-gathering vehicle. This took the form of a questionnaire that in the case of one cohort was administered half-way through the DL phase (i.e. six weeks into this part of the course), and in the case of the subsequent cohort immediately following completion of the DL phase during the first week of the direct contact phase. The aim of this deliberate variation in the timing of administration of the questionnaire was, of course, to establish any differences in participant reactions (albeit the reactions of different cohorts) at different points in time.

The questionnaires contained the following introduction and questions.

> There are some two hundred institutions in the U.K. offering short intensive courses of initial preparation for teachers of ESOL. Few of them employ a pre-course distance learning package and very few have a distance learning package as elaborate and lengthy as that of the TESOL Centre. As part of our routine course evaluation procedure, we would invite you to respond to the following questions.
>
> (1) Did you choose to take this course because it had a distance learning component?
> (2) How do you feel about the distance learning you have done?
> (3) Can you suggest any improvements either to the mechanism of our distance learning or to its content?
> (4) If you were designing this questionnaire is there any other vital question that should be asked and, if so, what is the answer?

Results from a questionnaire during the DL phase

Table 12.2 shows the responses of Cohort 1 (13 participants) to questions 1 and 2 in the questionnaire, the responses being roughly classified as positive, negative or mixed. As the table indicates, there was a reasonable predominance of positive responses and few overtly negative ones. Where responses were critical, they were generally constructively so.

Table 12.2 Responses to questionnaires administered during DL phase ($n = 13$)

Question	Positive	Mixed	Negative
1	10	1	2
2	7	6	—

Results from questionnaire after DL phase completed

The results of sampling carried out at the end of the DL phase on Cohort 2 (12 participants) correlate very closely with those of the mid-DL phase sample (Table 12.3). (For verbatim responses from the 12 course members in this cohort, see Appendix 12.2.)

Table 12.3 Responses to questionnaires administered after DL component completed ($n = 12$)

Question	Positive	Mixed	Negative
1	9	2	1
2	6	6	—

The sample size is relatively small and it must be recognised that the 12 respondents in this survey do not represent a balanced sample of our students. They are 12 out of the 19 starters on this course. The remaining 7 students either dropped out or deferred during the DL phase; their, presumably significant, views are not represented here. Similarly it cannot easily be ascertained how many people never got beyond the enquiry stage as a result of their discovery of the existence of a substantial DL requirement.

Results from a post-course questionnaire

The fourth category of evaluation was carried out by a further questionnaire administered at the end of the course in which course members were asked to reflect on the DL phase of the course as a complement to the course as a whole (Table 12.4). Questions elicited the degree of satisfaction or dissatisfaction that was felt in the areas of despatch, quality of content as a preparation for the direct contact phase, feedback from tutors and contact with the Centre.

Table 12.4 Responses to questionnaire administered at end of course ($n = 20$)

Question	Positive	Mixed	Negative
Despatch	20	—	—
Quality	18	1	1
Feedback	16	4	—
Contact	12	6	—

The responses from all four categories of feedback are summarised in Table 12.5.

Table 12.5 Summary of responses at various points of enquiry (rounded to nearest whole number)

Response to:	Nature of response		
	Positive (%)	Mixed (%)	Negative (%)
Feedback During DL Phase	89	8	3
Whole Experience *during* DL Phase	65	27	8
Whole Experience *after* DL Phase	63	33	4
Whole Experience *after Whole Course*	85	14	1

Conclusion

Feedback has been used to moderate tutor comment on participants' work and general as well as specific aspects of the DL materials in a move towards establishing a form of quality control mechanism. Though the sample numbers for the survey as a whole are relatively small, the results appear to be significant given that separate cohorts are represented. It is therefore possible to assert that the majority of people undertaking (and completing) a DL foundation programme in preparation for a face-to-face study block at initial teacher education level found the experience beneficial. The survey cannot account for those people who dropped out of the course or those who did not enrol for it upon finding that the course had a substantial DL element.

The evaluation exercise has involved the use of three different investigation techniques: feedback response slips, and two types of whole experience questionnaire. These have been administered at different points in the experience. The overall results summarised in Table 12.5 suggest that there is little to choose between the particular techniques or between timings for the investigations. Despite this negative finding, we have chosen to continue using all the techniques described on the grounds that the more feedback we have the better. However, there may well be interesting comparative results to be found by further surveys in these areas.

Appendix 12.1 Student response slip

TESOL CENTRE

Student Response Slip

Subject/unit _____ Module number _____

Please tick the boxes and/or give your views:

1)   I understand your comments   ☐

_____

_____

_____

2)   I agree with your comments   ☐

_____

_____

_____

3)   I agree with the grade   ☐

_____

_____

_____

Name _____ Course _____

Appendix 12.2 Questionnaire responses

1. **DID YOU CHOOSE TO TAKE THIS COURSE BECAUSE IT HAD A DISTANCE LEARNING COMPONENT?**

Generally Positive Answers

1.1 Yes, as I felt it would be a gentle ease into the course. Some of the assignments were quite challenging but at the same time enjoyable.

1.2 Yes. It was a way for me to get back into the feel for knowledge whilst remaining anonymous to all but myself.

1.3 Partially (a) enabled me to keep my job for a while. (b) thought it would give me a more in-depth training.

1.4 Main reason for taking course was that it was in Sheffield. But distance learning component did attract me to this course because it provides some background training before the residential teaching component.

1.5 Yes, it was an important consideration. I know people who have done straightforward 4 week courses — they said there was just too much to take in. I wanted to have a good grounding in the basics beforehand.

1.6 Yes, because I couldn't manage more than 4 weeks "away from home-base". I didn't really know quite how much the whole course involved but it seemed a good idea to have a foundation.

1.7 Yes, I felt that some background work was necessary before launching into an intensive course. I also felt I would enjoy some stimulation and a challenge whilst in Africa where books and materials are difficult to obtain.

1.8 The whole course appeared well structured and the distance learning element seemed to remove what, on four week intensive courses without d/l, would be "cramming".

1.9 Partly yes — living as I do in Sheffield I had the advantage of being able to use the library throughout the DLC. So I did choose the course in that it was a 16 week course effectively.

Mixed Answers

1.10 No and yes. No (because) I chose it because I was accepted to take it; yes, because it suited me best; being a teacher I could not afford too much time "out of work".

1.11 No — I found out about the distance learning afterwards. It was quite daunting to think of studying alone but turned out to be most enjoyable.

Negative Answers

1.12 No, I was not aware that the distance learning was a substitution for more intensive study at the Centre.

2.   HOW DO YOU FEEL ABOUT THE DISTANCE LEARNING YOU HAVE DONE?

Positive Answers

2.1 Quite pleased on the whole and very grateful for the incentive.

2.2 I have enjoyed it. Not being used to disciplined study-time at home, it has been a challenge. I still feel I have much to revise but the basics have "sunk in" — I hope!

2.3 In general I feel it has been very useful. It has made me feel more confident about tackling the teaching process.

2.4 Pleased with my results so far: made me feel that I had already learnt something before the residential block started.

2.5 Relieved. I feel that I've learnt a lot; particularly on the L.A. (Language Awareness) unit, I also enjoyed the phonetics as it was something totally new to me.

2.6 It has given me an insight into the required terminology. I feel better prepared to develop this over the four weeks.

Mixed Answers

2.7 The Background Reading and Phonetics seemed straightforward, however the grammar was at times most taxing.

2.8 Fairly positive, I don't remember all I did but then I do know more than I could have done without the DLC. It may put people off before the residential part!

2.9 All the distance learning was thought provoking, but there seemed to be many loose ends, particularly in Language Awareness. I suppose that it is the place of the residential block to draw the loose ends together.

2.10 I enjoyed the language awareness modules very much, also the phonetics. It was, though, working full time, difficult to find sufficient time to study.

2.11 I did feel that it progressed quite naturally and it became clearer through the modules. Module 1 of background reading & language awareness were rather daunting.

2.12 I have learned a lot, though I took a 4 week course in January 1990 with I.H. London (Introductory Course in TEFL) I was glad to cope with it.

3. CAN YOU SUGGEST ANY IMPROVEMENTS EITHER TO THE MECHANISM OF OUR DISTANCE LEARNING OR TO ITS CONTENT?

N.B. These responses are not classified but simply listed.

3.1 One thing keeps coming to mind about "phonetics" — it might seem a detail — I do not understand why some changes have been brought to the International system as if it was the International one .... I mean for 4 or 5 symbols .....

3.2 Not really. I found it demanding without making me feel inadequate.

3.3 In common with others I found "language awareness" the most difficult — lots of new terminology; but combined with the other 2 units it was palatable. The steady arrival of units through the post acted as a prompt. Phonetics via the tapes turned out to be fun, though increasingly difficult.

3.4 A more integrated approach might be more useful. Drawing together what has been learnt in all three modules.

3.5 Where possible give assessed questions without leaving a blank space below — possibly just suggest number of words/paragraphs needed instead. Alternatively give more questions of a more specific nature.

3.6 I felt that some of the questions were badly worded, the requests for information not being very clear. Would have preferred the assignments to be sent back sooner.

3.7 It was well produced and gave me confidence. I didn't like writing on dots! (background reading)

3.8 More instructions towards the language awareness unit.

3.9 I felt quite isolated really — this was a new method of learning and too dramatic a change from traditional methods. Some form of contact may be preferable.

3.10 I don't think that some of the very detailed questions in the Background Reading module were very useful — it seems that the general thrust, rather than numbers etc, is important. Otherwise no real complaints at all.

3.11 Perhaps more exposure to the variety of teaching materials available would have been useful. Was it necessary for the phonetics element to take up such a large proportion of the distance learning element?

3.12 Some modules took far longer to work through — intense thought and planning were required. The workload was not even but the content mostly was interesting and enjoyable. More practical advice needed for things like lesson plans.

4. IF YOU WERE DESIGNING THIS QUESTIONNAIRE IS THERE ANY OTHER VITAL QUESTION THAT SHOULD BE ASKED AND, IF SO, WHAT IS THE ANSWER?

N.B. Again responses to this question cannot usefully be classified. Not all 12 students responded.

4.1 **Q:** Did you find difficulty motivating yourself?
A: Initially, yes but then I got on a bit of a "roll" and started enjoying most of the work.

4.2 **Q:** Did you enjoy it?
A: Yes - most of the time.

4.3 **Q:** Did the component cover enough/too much/too little ground?
A: About right — possibly a bit more on actual teaching practice would be useful.

4.4   **Q:**   Did you stick to a rigid timetable, setting your own deadlines?
      A: No, I didn't and consequently was left with six to do in the last
              3 weeks. Deadlines set by the college may be an advantage for
              those of us lacking in discipline.

4.5   **Q:**   Would you do distance learning again?
      A: Yes, I enjoyed learning self-discipline and organisation at
              home!

4.6   **Q:**   Do you think you could have improved your planning of d/l
              to have completed this prior to the residential block?
      A: No. With the work I do I am surprised I achieved quite so
              much.

13 From Teaching Materials to Teacher Induction: A Progress Report

HÉLÈNE MULPHIN

Introduction

In 1991 the Open University (OU) established a Centre for Modern Languages to create a range of distance-learning courses for its undergraduate and associate[1] students and a series of study packs for the general public. The French materials, the first to be designed in the Centre, will endeavour to develop practical language skills and an awareness of French culture and society. When enrolling on *Ouverture*, the first course in the series (due to begin in February 1995), students will receive course books, audio and video cassettes and a study guide.

Tutors for this course will be recruited in October 1994 and in November they will receive a series of materials, some standard to OU courses in all disciplines, and others course specific, designed to guide them through the different steps of their OU tutorship.

This chapter will first define the principles underlying the writing of the course itself, which could be applied to the writing of any distance-learning material, and then give an overview of the specific tutor training needed in the context of distance learning with the OU, with particular reference to the distance-learning materials specially created for the staff development of language tutors.

The Tutorial in Print

One of the greatest challenges for the writers of a distance-learning course-book is to try to recreate the face-to-face experience, to achieve a 'tutorial in print'. The OU takes pride in having expertise in this area.

Developmental testing

As new course authors, the French team received advice from experienced members of other departments and were encouraged to read the publications of the OU's Institute of Educational Technology (IET), or relevant books such as Rowntree (1990). The materials we write go through a very thorough evaluation process: not only are they read and commented upon by internal members of the team, they are also sent to external critical readers at different stages of their production. In addition, they are tested on prospective students who supply detailed feedback through comprehensive questionnaires and interviews. The ensuing reports provide the basis for subsequent redrafts.

For the French team, it was interesting (and reassuring) to observe the close correspondence between the testers' reactions to the first unit of the course, as mentioned in the reports written by Kay Pole (1993), and various other members of IET, and the decisions, some inspired by IET (1985), the team had taken. Although we are dealing here with a language course, the principles outlined in Table 13.1 seem valid for any type of distance-learning course.

Self-assessed activities

The number of comments on activities received from the prospective students testing the materials reflects their status in the course. Indeed, the team has endeavoured to create a large number of self-assessed activities (with clear and constructive feedback) in order to fulfil a series of purposes, as outlined by Grant (1984):

(1) to overcome the distance-learner isolation (by extending the 'tutorial in print' and establishing a virtual student/tutor dialogue), thus reducing anxiety;
(2) to promote active learning (by interrupting passive reading and requiring the student's constant involvement);
(3) to test the command of learning objectives;
(4) to help self-diagnosis and remediation;
(5) to give the student responsibility for his/her own learning.

The nature of a language course dictates some of the decisions taken regarding activities (e.g. making sure that each one of them has a communicative purpose) but other resolutions, such as systematically asking students for a response involving their personal experience, can apply to all distance courses.

Table 13.1 Comparison of decisions made by writing team and reactions of developmental testers

Decisions taken by the team	Developmental testers particularly liked
When writing, imagine the student is beside you, and talk directly to him/her	being addressed personally and directly
Sentences should be short and simple; all technical terms should be defined and used accurately and consistently	the natural style and the use of everyday language
Be generous with introductory sessions; use organisers to provide a rationale for the choice of topics and to convince students of the usefulness and relevance of the activities suggested; state objectives clearly	knowing where they were going
Give an estimate of the average study time required and tell students to interpret this in the light of their own natural speed	the indication of approximate timing given for each activity (although often underestimated by the team)
Take into account the ability range among students, and the variation in levels of concentration in one individual	the variations in levels of difficulty
Provide plenty of variety to maintain interest and to offer students a temporary respite from components that are heavy going	the mix of media and wide range of types of activities
Keep students actively involved	the large number of activities
Anticipate students' reactions and pre-empt them	the feedback given for each activity, including models for open-ended activities

In order to be valuable, feedback must be immediate, clear, and must provide remedial teaching for those students who fail to give a correct answer. It must also contain a model answer in the case of open-ended exercises. These characteristics too can apply to all distance courses.

The first unit contained optional activities. These were quite popular with students; the more advanced took them in their stride, the others planned to come back to them if time was available. Unfortunately, space constraints have precluded their use in the final version of the first course. However, the possibility of including optional activities is being considered for subsequent courses, which at the moment are still at the planning stage.

Lay-out

In preparing the first draft it was not possible to implement some of the decisions the team had made concerning layout. It was interesting to see that some of the students' spontaneous comments indicated that they felt the same way as the team. In particular they advocated the use of icons and of a second colour to increase accessibility. Colour was especially recommended for the pages containing the 'Corrigé', which the students agreed should not be just after the activity but at a safe distance, preventing the temptation to look up answers too quickly. All these decisions will be taken account of in the final version.

On the other hand, students recommended the provision of space inside the activity to write in their own answers. The team had received the opposite advice on the assumption that many students would not want to deface their course-book, in order to be able to sell it after completing the course.

Access to equipment and length of study sessions are two major issues for OU students: for instance they might have to compete for the use of the video recorder with other members of the family; or they might plan to make use of valuable time on their way to and from work. The study-chart, which precedes each unit of work and provides at a glance a framework for study sessions proved to be a popular feature. (See Table 13. 2 for an example.)

Table 13.2 One of the suggested models for a study chart

Topic	Activity	Medium	Approximate study time	Main teaching point
6. Christmas in the ward	Activities 1-9	Audio + book	2hrs 30	
6.1 The matron	1. Listening for gist	Audio	10 minutes	Expressing disappointment
	2. Listening for detailed comprehension (gap-filling)	Audio + book	15 minutes	Percentages the imperfect tense
6.2 Drastic cutbacks	3. Reading comprehension	Book	15 minutes	Expressions of time

The study guide

Undergraduates enrolling on the French course will receive a specially designed study guide to help them acquire distance-learning study skills and provide them with support in language-specific learning skills, such as how to recognize their own learning behaviour, and benefit from it. It will also explain what tutors will expect of students, and what students are entitled to expect from their tutor, both at a distance (for example, written or over-the-telephone feedback on their progress) and during face-to-face tutorials.

Tutorials

The French programme will offer 18 hours of group tutorials organised by the Regions, and although face-to-face tutorials are not compulsory, in view of possible geographical or physical difficulties, a large number of students is expected to attend and to benefit from the opportunity to practise their skills in a communicative context.

Tutor Training

Tutor recruitment for the first French course will take place in October 1994. The information received by the applicant states: 'You should be a graduate in French, or the equivalent, with extensive teaching experience, preferably of adults. You should be committed to comunicative language-teaching strategies, and be aware of the particular problems of teaching language at a distance.' After receiving a brief explanation about tutorials and assignments, applicants are also informed that they will be expected to be available by telephone to help students with their difficulties, and that some formal tuition and assessment may also be carried out by telephone.

In November those selected will be sent the OU standard publication for new tutors (*Open Teaching*), the French course material, and the course-specific Tutor Notes and marking schemes. In addition the Regions will organise role-based induction, which is standard practice for all new OU tutors, and course-based briefing sessions, based on the materials of the tutor pack L900, *Open Learning in Languages: A Guide for Tutors*, which is to be published in October 1994.

Once they start in February 1995 the work of the new tutors will be monitored by the Regions and the course team. Apart from checking whether the mark given for an assignment is in the right range, the course team will pay particular attention to the comments and feedback supplied to the student with the returned assignment.

Open Teaching and the Open Teaching File

Prepared by members of the OU Staff Development Team, *Open Teaching* sets out to explain to the new tutor the uniqueness of the experience of teaching for the OU: it emphasises the openness of the admission system, the particular nature of the students (adult, part-time) and the implications of correspondence tuition, stressing the fact it is a student-led exchange. *Open Teaching* also gives guidance about organising oneself throughout the OU year, counselling students, and face-to-face tuition.

Open Teaching is complemented by the Open Teaching File, a briefing document on administrative procedures and the role of the tutor. The File has been designed as a ring-binder, allowing information to be updated at any time.

The Centre for Modern Languages will also produce a pack of materials that are intended to support and train its tutors, but that will be generic enough to be of interest to all language tutors. This tutor pack will be directed at individual tutors but will contain supplementary material for tutor trainers. It is planned to include:

- general theories of language teaching;
- general techniques to facilitate learning;
- self-evaluation checklists such as those mentioned by Ashton *et al.* (1981);
- a 30-minute video cassette;
- a one-hour audio cassette.

The video will show examples of classroom teaching, filmed unrehearsed, but after several meetings between the Centre and the tutors involved. The audio tape will contain interviews with students and tutors describing their experiences, including interviews with students who have attended an intensive day. It will also deal with telephone tuition. A small booklet will show how the audio-visual material may be exploited during tutor training sessions.

Telephone tutoring

The telephone plays an important role in OU courses, and advice on telephone tutoring/counselling has been built into the tutor training programme. The following points would seem to be relevant:

- visual support is vital; tutors should ensure that they post/fax material ahead, and that they have reference works to hand;
- problems of sound definition should be compensated for (e.g. by saying things slowly and very intelligibly, by repeating);

- names should be used to ensure participation;
- tutors should be realistic about the amount of material it is possible to cover in the time;
- body-language cannot be used (e.g. to trigger the memory) and tutors should compensate for this;
- telephone tutoring is a very tiring experience and the concentration span is shorter.

Telephone counselling

As well as imparting educational guidance, OU tutors often have to provide personal counselling to students experiencing problems or going through a crisis. For some people isolation may reduce anxiety, for others it may well create pressure. Watts (1979) mentions that tutors are expected to be able to identify and pursue the individual problems of their students. They are encouraged to develop a trusting and friendly relationship with students, to show sympathy and empathy. Therefore they themselves need guidance in the performance of the affective side of their role.

Below are some examples of advice relating to the affective domain:

- highlight the positive, boost morale;
- show sympathy and empathy repeatedly; reassure;
- personalise the approach;
- listen carefully to clues (e.g. tone of voice);
- keep the conversation going until you reach a mutually satisfactory conclusion;
- summarise the conclusions;
- finish constructively/on a high note.

Many of these recommendations apply to face-to-face tuition, but they become crucial in telephone tutoring. In a sense, everything seems to be magnified by the medium.

Conclusion

Tutors on the OU French course will be experienced teachers but will probably be new to distance teaching. By using distance-learning materials, and by contacting their Staff Tutors for advice, OU tutors studying with the pack will effectively anticipate their students' experience. The delivery process is in itself therefore an important element in their training, since they are thereby more likely to achieve understanding of the problems and difficulties that these students will face.

Note

1. Associate students are those who do not intend to complete a degree, but who wish to study for a certificate or diploma or simply take one or two courses which interest them.

References

Ashton, P., Hunt, P., Jones, S. and Watson, G. (1981) *Curriculum in Action: Practical Classroom Evaluation.* Milton Keynes: Open University.

Grant, J. (1984) *Self-assessment and Self-remediation Strategies.* Milton Keynes: IET, Open University.

IET. (1985) *Making Self-instructional Materials.* Milton Keynes: IET, Open University.

Pole, K. (1993) *Developmental Testing Report, Prototype Unit L220.* Milton Keynes: IET, Open University.

Rowntree, D. (1990) *Teaching Through Self-instruction.* London: Kogan Page.

Watts, G. (1979) Personal counselling in the Open University. *Teaching at a Distance* 15, 21–26.

14 *Formation à Distance* — Learning Strategies

BEVERLEY HALLAM

Project Context and Rationale

The National Curriculum in Modern Languages (1992) introduced to schools the compulsory study of at least one foreign language by all pupils aged 11 to 16, working to a specified programme with attainment targets. This has had a major impact on language departments, seriously affecting both teachers and pupils. The new programme has altered the aims of language courses in a way that requires a new style of teaching; in particular, the use of the target language as the primary vehicle for classroom communication has significant implications for the linguistic competence of the teacher.

Modern Language Departments have often contained one or more staff teaching a language in which they are not specialists and even ones with no language qualifications at all. Such teachers, faced with delivering most of a 35- or 70-minute lesson in the target language are, quite understandably, experiencing a crisis of confidence in their ability. In addition to this, for the first time in many schools, teachers are having to teach learners of all abilities which, by necessity, affects the kinds of activity undertaken in the classroom, as well as the whole methodological ethos.

Finally, the policy of a language for all has created the problem of recruiting and training some 3,000 extra modern-languages teachers.

The *Formation à Distance* Project, directed by Mike Buckby at the University of York, and Barry Jones at Homerton College, Cambridge, came into being to try to address some of these difficulties, by producing a set of professional development materials for teachers of French, which had the flexibility to be used by the individual working alone or by groups of teachers as departmental in-service education and training (INSET). The project was funded by the French Embassy who were concerned to help bring about an improvement in the quality of French teaching, and by the Department for Education (DFE), who were concerned about the difficulties in teacher recruitment. The materials are published and distributed by Collins Educational.

At the beginning of the project, research carried out by the project team together with the DFE estimated that some 3,000 additional qualified modern-language teachers were needed to implement the National Curriculum successfully. To try to help remedy this, the first phase of the project involved the devising of a set of materials that would propose a general methodological and linguistic approach to the teaching of French in secondary schools, in order to help teachers to meet the demands of the National Curriculum with enjoyment and success. The materials are intended in the first instance for qualified language teachers who left the classroom some years ago; very often, these are women who left teaching anything up to ten years ago to bring up their own families, and are now considering a return to the profession. However, when one thinks of the enormous changes that modern-language teaching has undergone, even in the last five years, it is not difficult to imagine the trepidation and lack of confidence experienced by these returning teachers. Sweeping changes in examinations, methodology, use of target language, staffroom terminology, assessment, and the advent of new ideas such as profiling and Records of Achievement, all contribute to the confusion of the returner and become obstacles to their return.

As well as for this group, the materials are also very useful for conventional face-to-face teaching for students in initial teacher training and are ideally suited for use by language departments as ongoing departmental INSET.

Why Distance Training?

The project team geared the package of materials to a distance-training approach for both practical and philosophical reasons. At the practical level, it is often difficult for an intending returner to attend a formal training course because of lack of child-care facilities, or financial and transport difficulties. It is also increasingly difficult for teachers in post to be released from schools for INSET. These materials, therefore, offer the opportunity for the user to work in depth, but flexibly, whenever time allows, and are suitable either for the person working alone or for groups working together.

The distance-training approach, however, also accords well with the emphasis given in the National Curriculum documents to autonomy in language learning and the increasing trend to encouraging self-directed and flexible learning. Teachers who have experienced this approach in their own training are more likely to be able to facilitate and encourage the same in their learners and all teachers should, like their students, be able to specify their own aims and draw up action plans for achieving them. They should also be given the means regularly to assess and evaluate their teaching performance. These materials show modern-language teachers how they can take responsibility for their own professional development, from setting their own aims to drawing up action plans to meet these aims and then going on to assess and evaluate their progress. In an era of change in education generally, it is no longer possible for the teacher to believe that an initial short period of training is going to sustain classroom practice and professional development throughout an entire career. The materials described below provide modern-language teachers with a means of reviewing and evaluating their own teaching performance and of studying, at times convenient to them, the successful teaching strategies of others.

A Framework for Teaching

The *Learning Strategies* materials (Buckby, Jones & Berwick, 1992), do not propose a single, definitive method of teaching. It is not possible, at present, for us to say that any single theory as to how a learner acquires a foreign language has provided a complete and wholly satisfactory explanation of the process, and it is therefore dangerous to base a methodology on too narrow and prescriptive a method. It would seem to be safer and more sensible to take an eclectic approach to this question, as it often appears that modern-language teaching has suffered greatly in the past from violent swings of the methodological pendulum. The project team was keen to build a reasoned and thoughtful structure to provide users of the materials with a solid, pragmatic basis on which to construct an individual teaching method, with which they and their pupils would feel comfortable and that would make language teaching and learning successful and enjoyable. The practical structure that is proposed as a way to manage teaching and learning is based on both research and experience, and consists of a progression of eight clear stages or steps.

The Learning Steps

Step 1 — Setting appropriate learning goals

Successful learning and teaching depend on the definition of goals and aims, both short and long term. Learning is goal-orientated. The learners must see the aims as sensible, achievable, valid, and meaningful for them. It is also vital that these goals are frequently achieved, and that this success is monitored by frequent checks and assessments.

Step 2 — Meeting and understanding the language

This step comprises two strands. Firstly, the learners meet new language, either orally or written, for the first time. They must learn to recognise the words, learn not to confuse them with others that look or sound similar, and understand them in context. When the learners can do this with ease and confidence, they are ready to progress on to the next steps. Secondly, it is important to recognise that listening and reading are important skills in their own right. Considerable opportunities should be provided for purposeful reading and listening activities, as these are crucial in the acquisition of a foreign language.

Step 3 — Imitation

Having heard and read the new words many times, the learners pronounce them for the first time. They imitate immediately after a model, such as the teacher, the cassette or the video, as well as they are able. Imitation may also be copying a written model from the board, the overhead projector, or a book. Here again, it is essential that the learner brings thought and understanding to this learning step, if motivation and enjoyment are not to diminish.

Step 4 — Repetition

In order to appreciate fully the distinction between imitation and repetition, it is important to bear in mind that words stay in the short-term memory for between only three and ten seconds. Step 4 involves the learners in working to transfer new words from the short-term memory to the long-term memory. They say a word or a phrase that they have previously heard and imitated many times, but now without an immediate model, basing their utterances on memory. The time gap gradually increases from a minute or two to an hour or two, then days, weeks, and months. Repetition also involves writing key sentences in a variety of ways and without an immediate printed or written model.

Step 5 — Understanding patterns in language

At this stage, the learners will be able to look carefully at the sentences they have met, imitated and repeated. With help, they will be able to see, and to express in their own words, the principles, patterns or rules that underlie the sentences. The understanding they derive from this exercise will enable learners to proceed to Steps 6 and 7.

Step 6 — Manipulation

At this stage, guided by the teacher or the materials, the learners begin to make new combinations with known language in closely structured situations. They combine new grammatical points with familiar vocabulary, and vice versa. This important step merits a good proportion of the available time.

Step 7 — Production and creativity

This stage represents the ultimate goal for the learners, and it is important that they reach it right from the start of their language course. Here, they exploit their ability to manipulate and re-combine known language to produce new utterances, in which they might express their own ideas and opinions. They should be able to do this, for example, in a natural conversation, role plays, games and writing, where the emphasis is on the ideas expressed rather than on the words and structures used. What distinguishes creative work is that it is based primarily on the ideas to be expressed and is not closely controlled linguistically.

Step 8 — Assessment and evaluation

For the learning process to be effective, regular and frequent assessment is essential. This allows the learners to evaluate their own success in achieving certain goals, which should be a positive experience, with success breeding success. However, assessment should be followed by evaluation. Having examined the results provided by the assessment, the learners, with the guidance of the teacher, decide on their future action. If the evidence is positive, the learner will then formulate new goals to aim for. If there are found to be problems, support strategies must be devised, such as doing certain exercises again or doing extra ones. In the longer term, the results of assessment can be used to help both teachers and learners to replace inefficient teaching and learning techniques by ones that are both more successful and more enjoyable.

To sum up, therefore, the proposed teaching and learning sequence consists of setting clear objectives, producing a comprehensive action plan to achieve these, assessment of the extent to which the plan has worked and appropriate evaluation. This framework makes no pretensions to being an accurate psychological model of how a language is learnt, but aims instead to provide a pragmatic structure, based on successful practice, on which teachers can base their work.

The Materials

The materials produced by the project team are divided into two parts: *Learning Strategies*, which is the professional development course described above, and *Stratégies*, which are materials for use in the classroom and that put into the practice the theoretical aspects described in *Learning Strategies*.

Learning strategies

The video

There is a video that contains four 20-minute programmes; these were originally broadcast on Channel 4 in Spring of 1992. They show some 20 teachers in comprehensive schools from different socio-economic areas of England and Wales teaching French enjoyably and successfully to pupils of all ages and abilities. Each programme explores two of the Learning Steps described above.

The teachers' manual

The Manual is organised into eight main sections, each one concerned with one of the eight steps in the proposed framework describing the language-learning process. Each section is then divided into three parts: Before viewing, While viewing, and After viewing. While working on the manual, the teachers follow the same learning steps as they will use with their pupils.

The 'Before viewing' sections contain a discussion of some of the theoretical background to the Step, combined with practical teaching suggestions, designed as preparation for watching the video.

The 'While viewing' sections contain discussion, and some guided activities, to help users gain the maximum benefit from watching the video. Finally, the 'After viewing' sections contain suggestions for activities designed to focus attention on the main points which the video illustrates, and to help teachers adapt the ideas and techniques to suit their own teaching.

The authors, mindful that many of the users of the materials will be working alone at home, recommend a series of procedures for working on each of the Learning Steps. The first of these procedures involves the setting up of clear goals and objectives for the user to achieve by the end of a given chapter, mirroring the cardinal importance given to the setting up of clear goals for the pupil in the classroom situation. Copious activities and tasks are set out for the learner to do both before and while watching the video, activities that also aim to train the teacher in the techniques of lesson observation, including observation of their own lessons. In the After viewing section, users are encouraged to work on ways of developing the ideas and techniques presented, and consider how they can best be adapted to suit their own situations and teaching styles, and how alternative techniques could be devised. Finally, as the proposed framework suggests should be the case in the classroom, users are asked to make use of the assessment at the end of each section to measure the extent to which their goals have been achieved. An evaluation should then be made based on this evidence, and a decision taken as to what to do next.

To allow teachers further scope for reflection on their practice, lessons in Russian have been included in the manual. For those for whom Russian is an unknown language, these lessons provide valuable insights into the difficulties and pleasures of learning a new language, and can help teachers enormously in their understanding of what is and what is not useful in language learning.

Audio cassettes

The third element in the package of materials is two audio cassettes, which contain interviews with the teachers who appear on the video, speaking about the various techniques, strategies and methodology that they use in the classroom. The project team felt that it was most important to hear the thoughts and opinions of the teachers themselves, who go unheard all too often when theoretical questions are being discussed. The cassettes also have the function of providing teachers with some linguistic help in regard to use of the target language in the classroom.

Stratégies

The project team was particularly keen that the theoretical aspects of methodology discussed in the *Learning Strategies* materials should be clearly demonstrated at a more practical level. Thus, *Stratégies* was developed for teachers to use with learners in the classroom, thereby establishing a link between theory and practice. Although the *Learning*

Strategies materials themselves are rich in suggestions, ideas and practical advice for the classroom teacher, *Stratégies* takes this a little further.

The users are shown how the principles and techniques studied and worked on in *Learning Strategies* are put into practice. The *Stratégies* package contains two videos, a Teachers' Guide, and a set of Copymaster Activity sheets for use with pupils.

The videos

The guiding principle in the making of the videos was that the end result could be viewed with pleasure by French youngsters. The six 25-minute TV programmes on the videos deal with subjects and situations that would be of interest to young teenagers, without being too difficult linguistically. Filmed on location in Créteil, the programmes deal with various aspects of French life, and contain numerous examples of transactional and creative language use. The pupil-viewers are presented with new and exciting situations and information, and they also see practical demonstrations of how to do and make things. In order not to overtax the learner, the programmes are divided into several sections that may be worked on independently, and that last only three or four minutes each.

The copymasters

As an accompaniment to the videos, the activity sheets offer teachers and learners a method of putting into practice the principles and learning steps expounded in *Learning Strategies* and, following its model, the pupils are asked to do certain activities before, during, and after watching the video. The approach to language is a communicative one, given that one of the main objects of the project is the encouragement of the successful implementation of the National Curriculum. The activities all have a definite and authentic aim and the language used is authentic. The materials also lend themselves to the development of pupil autonomy, as required by the National Curriculum.

The Teachers' Guide

Finally, this manual offers suggestions as to how teachers can best make use of the videos and the pupils' material. It also contains complete transcripts of all the television programmes shown on the video.

An Intensive Course in France

Although a thorough and thoughtful approach to the learning–teaching framework can help towards smoothing the path to re-entry to the classroom for returners, it cannot by itself improve their linguistic competence, which is very often one of their principal concerns. To solve this difficulty, users of the materials could apply to participate in an intensive two-week course at the University of Nancy in July of 1993. It was planned that applicants should receive teaching all in French, as well as being given projects to finish by the end of the course, and the collecting and ordering of realia for use in the preparation of their own lessons. However, the team was forced, with great regret, to cancel the course in early June as, despite widespread advertising in the national and specialist press, we received insufficient applications from suitably qualified people to make the course viable. It was both surprising and disappointing that such an opportunity, with almost full funding for participants, should have to be cancelled due to a lack of response.

The Support Networks

It was realised at the beginning of the project that, if the *Learning Strategies* professional development course was to be completely successful, it was going to be necessary to try to establish support networks to which users could go for help and advice should they need it. In this way, teachers could get in touch with fellow users of the materials, and exchange ideas and suggestions on issues of methodology and even classroom management. In order that these networks might continue to function after the project has ended, it was essential to find organisations that had some durability in the present changing and uncertain atmosphere that surrounds education.

For this reason, it was seen as unrealistic to expect LEA Modern-Language Advisers, Inspectors, and Initial Teacher Training establishments to act as network centres. Instead, it was decided to base the networks around the recently instituted Comenius Centres[1] that would hold copies of the materials for people to consult, and we hoped that many other language organisations such as branches of the Association for Language Learning (ALL) would also be in a position to contribute to the network. In order to help network centres to assist users of the package, the project team put together a manual entitled *Recruiting and Retraining Modern Language Teachers for the National Curriculum.* This has now been published, and contains information, advice and suggestions as to how potential returners in a given area can be reached, supported, and helped successfully back into the classroom. As all schools in England and Wales introduce the teaching of a language for all pupils until the age of 16, the demand for trained and well-qualified language teachers will steadily increase, and our hope is that the manual will be of some assistance to network centres and schools, particularly governing bodies, in this respect.

The project team has also set up the possibility for users of the materials to communicate with each other electronically, by means of the Campus 2000 facility. In this way, it was hoped initially that users, even if they were living a long way from large centres of population, would be able to seek support from colleagues in schools either at a local or a wider level. Indeed, it was planned that, ultimately, users would have access to international electronic networks such as the Edu 2000 network, and the one established by the Commission de l'Europe de l'Ouest de la Fédération Internationale des Professeurs de Français, co-ordinated in the UK by Mike Buckby at the University of York. It would be ideal in the longer term if encouraging teachers in this way to use information technology led to an increased awareness of its potential in the classroom.

However, the organisation of the support networks has presented a series of problems that may be of interest to those planning similar materials in the future. As well as the difficulties of our planned network centres lacking the finance and facilities to assist users as they would like, this final phase of the project has been thwarted by two very specific difficulties that relate to the distribution of the materials and the timescale. The project is due to end at the end of August 1993, leaving no one available to manage any electronic conferencing or communication that might take place once users have had time to familiarise themselves with the materials. The materials themselves were published in October 1992 by Collins Educational, who were in charge of their marketing, distribution, and sale. In contrast to most other distance training schemes, therefore, the producers of the materials, that is, the project team, have not been responsible for their distribution, which has made the finding and follow-up support of users very difficult. Finally, it may be that the principal difficulty lies with the group for whom the materials were mainly designed, the returners. By definition, these people are not in schools but in their own homes, and therefore hard to target.

It is as yet far too early to make any kind of conclusive evaluation or assessment of the success of the materials. As mentioned above, the packages were published in October of 1992, and users of the materials with whom we are in touch only began to work methodically through the course at the beginning of 1993. However, the responses that we have had so far are very positive. Individual users working alone at home have mentioned the flexibility of study that this kind of course has not only in terms of time, but also in approach, in that they feel that they are able to concentrate and work on their particular needs and weaknesses. The materials have been very successful in a face-to-face context, as a part of conventional teacher training and INSET, and Returners' Courses run by LEAs. At least three LEAs, two in England and one in Wales (Clwyd), have used the materials as part of a Returners' Course, and feedback from all has been very encouraging. To evaluate fully the success of the project solely as a Distance Training scheme, and not for any of the materials it has produced, would require more time and funding. It would be interesting, a few years hence, to try to establish how many French teachers it has helped back into the classroom.

Note

1. The Comenius network (of centres) is an initiative of the Centre for Information on Language Teaching and Research (CILT), and was developed in partnership with designated host institutions and with the full support of central government. It brings together all the national agencies working in the field of languages, together with European cultural institutes. (See Comenius: The broadsheet of the Comenius network. Issue 1, October 1993.)

Reference

Buckby, M., Jones, B. and Berwick, G. (1992) *Learning Strategies*. London: Collins.

15 Concepts of Quality in Distance Education

DAVID CARVER

In this chapter I want to focus more on the concept of distance education, and less on that of language teaching, partly because I see distance education as the basic area of concern, and partly because I do not see the relationship between distance education and language teaching, or teacher education for language teaching, as being essentially different from the corresponding relationship in respect of any other content area. This claim I return to later.

The Nature of Distance Education

The most apparent and surface manifestation of distance education is that the student is not present at an institution, and that teaching is conducted by means of correspondence material and/or electronic media. From this fact emerges a very strong tendency for distance education to be *industrialised.* This concept was introduced by Otto Peters (discussed in Keegan, 1990: ch. 5); Peters lists a number of features of industrial production that can be utilised without any sense of strain in characterising distance education: among them division of labour, mechanisation, scientific control, mass production, and centralisation. These characteristics result very understandably from the physical facts of distance education. Over and beyond that, they also constitute part of a set of values that, when Peters was writing, might have seemed peculiar to distance education.

It seems to me now not unrealistic to see education as a whole strongly influenced by values derived from industry and even more from the management of industry (one thinks of concepts such as quality assurance, total quality care, performance targets, delivery, corporate plans, competitive tendering). Within this framework, distance education can be seen as no longer a marginal activity offering second-chance and third-age courses but as, at its best, a paradigm case of good practice, at the leading edge of educational development.

To slightly over-dramatise this point, I list below some characteristic features of distance education, which come very naturally from the very fact of physical separation; these features are contrasted with some possible features of contact education. These latter features are possible in a weak sense; they could occur, but they may not normally do so, and they sit uneasily within the managerial framework. I list them as a way of marking out an alternative framework (Table 15.1).

Table 15.1 Comparison of distance and contact education

Distance *probable features*	*Contact* *possible features*
— packages	— libraries/bookshops/reading lists/bibliographies
— purpose-made materials	— authentic texts
— individual study	— group activities
— predetermined content and outcomes; an attempt to control process through design of activities.	— negotiated content, process and outcomes
— an institutional base	— personal relationships among students and between teachers and learners
— summative assessment	— formative assessment
— judgemental role of institution	— collaborative roles of learners and teachers
— directed programme	— exploratory study
— assignment oriented	— process oriented
— focus on skills and knowledge	— focus on skills, knowledge, and attitudes
— driven by administration and design of the programme	— driven by teaching and learning
— periodic review of design	— on-going revision of content and process
— quality assurance and accountability	— learner autonomy

Quality (1)

Within the managerial framework one can describe with some confidence the nature of quality assurance for distance education. The overarching principles as elsewhere are *economy*, *efficiency*, and *effectiveness*, the three Es (Adams, 1991: 7). Each of the characteristic features of distance education can be operationalised in terms of good practice: for instance there is research available on optimum print size; there is evidence that the provision of collections of readings promotes student effort more than the provision of a study guide alone (Jevons, 1984: 32, cited in Holmberg, 1989: 67); individual study can be expressed in terms of standard student effort hours; learning outcomes can be expressed in terms of testable competencies; performance indicators such as delivery time, drop-out rate, completion time, can be applied (Loder, 1990); exacting quality control procedures (Yorke, 1992) can be applied to the production and on-going monitoring of the product; the product will be vigorously marketed within the corporate plan; it will represent the company's corporate image, and it will be reviewed in terms of the end of year trading account; the quality of the whole enterprise will be confirmed by the bestowal of BS5750[1].

I am slightly exaggerating the concept (but only very slightly), but the industrial and managerial approach to quality assurance here delineated is strongly established, and it cannot simply be ignored because it represents an uncomfortable paradigm shift for academics who grew up in another value system. In itself it represents a coherently articulated and persuasively presented framework for the definition and evaluation of quality in education.

I want now to pick at some possible areas of weakness in the paradigm, in order to outline a less-well-articulated alternative.

Distance Education and Open Learning

The discomfort mentioned above is perhaps particularly acute in the area of distance education, and is indicated for instance in arguments that relate distance education to open learning, with slogans such as *Beyond Distance Teaching — Towards Open Learning* (Hodgson, Mann & Snell, 1987).

This move in the debate can be based on the distinction between distance education as a delivery system and open learning as a philosophy of education. It is not the case however that the delivery system can simply be filled with any one of several acceptable philosophies. Rowntree (1992: 13) points out that there is a potential conflict between the method and the philosophy of open learning, which can be summarised in Table 15.2.

Table 15.2 Method and philosophy of open learning (derived from Rowntree, 1992: 13)

Method	Philosophy
— packaged learning	— focus on the learner
— activities	— focus on the context
— mass-produced study guides	— belief in self-direction and individual variation
— variety of media	— aim of autonomy
— well-designed materials	
— systematic planning	

More fundamentally, as I have argued, the delivery system is not neutral, but strongly implies in itself a value-laden ideology.

Boot & Hodgson (1987: 8) analyse what they see as two orientations to open learning (Table 15.3).

Table 15.3 Orientations to open learning

Tradition A Dissemination	Tradition B Development
— knowledge as a commodity	— learning as a process
— individualisation	— the growth of autonomy
— cafeteria: choice	— self-catering: planning menus and experimenting with recipes
— study skills	— learning strategies
— public standards	— negotiation and collaboration

The tension between these two orientations is encapsulated in a striking quotation from the International Higher Education Standing Committee (IHESC) reported by Boot & Hodgson (1988: 200):

> Those involved in open learning undertake the learning of subject matter at their own pace and without direct supervision, unhindered by the severe time pressures normally experienced in classroom situations. Within overall time constraints, they permit learners to travel the educational road at their own pace. Open learning programmes must be delivered as highly structured units of material, so that learners are able to pursue their learning activities along a clearly defined and directed pathway.

The two authors comment: 'It is tempting to equate the use of the word "open" in this passage with its use in the term "open-prison" '(Boot & Hodgson, 1988: 200).

Vocational Training

Concepts like 'clearly defined and directed pathways', and 'highly structured planning' match with the vocational and training orientation of the managerial framework. National Vocational Qualifications (NVQs) and their Scottish analogues (SVQs) are increasingly influencing teacher education with the resurrection of competency-based teacher-training programmes. McNamara (1992) reminds us that competency-based teacher-training during the previous periods when it was in vogue was tested and found wanting even by its most ardent advocates. However, the competency movement has re-emerged with some concern to avoid the mistakes of the past. Burke (1992) outlines a research-degree programme in the field of NVQs. Here again, then, quality assurance procedures can be applied to distance education, with the demand for specification of testable NVQ-like outcomes of course units.

Three recent papers present a penetrating critique of the NVQ model. Marshall (1991) argues that the model could actually discourage the development of qualities that are highly relevant to vocational training but that are not easily operationalised (such as flexibility, curiosity, imagination). More fundamentally perhaps, because the model is posited on a narrow performance rather than competence basis, it actually diverts attention away from the cognitive and attitudinal processes which underlie performance. (McGarvey & Swallow (1986) make a comparable criticism of classical skills-based microteaching.)

In contrast to the behaviourist view of the NVQ model, Hodkinson (1992) offers an interactionist model of competence, in which observable performance is seen in relation both to underlying cognitive processes and to schemata for action, and also in relation to the immediate situation and the cultural context. He speaks of rescuing the potentially valuable concept of competence from its behaviouristic fetters (op. cit.: 38). Muller and Funnell (1992) reinterpret the concept of quality in vocational formation, and argue that this concept must be retrieved from the managers and restored to the practitioners. They conclude their paper:

> It is our view that at the heart of the delivery of quality is the role played by the learner in **determining**, **controlling**, **creating**, and **managing** the learning experience. This view, which offers a substantial challenge to aspects of traditional practice in vocational education and training, accords with the tenets of TQM^2 and supports the liberal educational notions underpinning student autonomy. (p. 260)

In the same spirit, Boot & Hodgson (1988) argue that the divide between method and philosophy in open learning is unnecessary, and ultimately untenable. Methods are necessarily methods for attaining goals. Some of the recent discussion of NVQs (and SVQs), central concepts in managerialist methodology, present a case for seeing this methodology as ineffective. Therefore there can be no interest in discussing the quality of ineffective methodology, except perhaps an aesthetic interest akin to that of Matthew Arnold sighing over the University of Oxford as the home of lost causes and impossible dreams.

Counselling

A difficult and untidy area for the managerial approach is that of student counselling. It is frustrating and the cause of inefficiency that students do not always play their allotted part in the rational plan, but instead display irrational behaviour, miss deadlines, have emotional crises, and are sometimes out of key with the plan. Snell (1987) suggests that the main managerialist strategies in the area of the affective domain are to attempt to prevent, mask, or soothe painful and unpleasant emotions on the part of students. Other familiar responses are to routinise counselling provision by restricting it to procedures such as advising on choice of course units, or to reroute student problems to specialist agents such as the medical department. Snell contrasts these strategies with the more risky strategy of what he calls 'working with and through feelings'. Although it is risky, Snell argues that this strategy may be important for its potential contribution to further learning and development (p. 69).

A number of writers (Kaye & Rumble, 1981: 13; Keegan, 1986: 197;

Grugeon, 1987: 198; Holmberg, 1989: 123) emphasise the importance of a student support system that is complementary to the design and delivery systems. Grugeon quotes with approval the view that academic counselling should not restrict itself to a therapeutic or ameliorative role, but should seek to engage the student in a critical dialogue.

Holmberg (1989: 112–15) provides an excellent summary of current views on good practice in academic counselling; his statement of theory for distance education includes an emphasis on the centrality of the factors of warmth in personal relations, pleasure in studying, empathy between students and staff — a task for academic counselling is to foster these qualities. I suggest also that academic counselling should include more explicit provision for cognitive and metacognitive development of the learner, of the kind that in language teaching we have come to call learner training (Oxford, 1990; Dickinson, 1992). (This kind of approach I take to be over and beyond the conventional study skills training, which focuses on technical aspects of study.)

Teaching and Learning

Learning conceptualised as anything other than the outcome of competent teaching sits awkwardly in a managerial framework. I am thinking here of factors such as motivation, individual differences, learner styles and strategies, cognitive and metacognitive competence, factors that are not easily amenable to prior planning of process and outcomes. One line of attack would be to seek ever more sophisticated teaching strategies aimed at enabling the programme designers to reach the intended outcomes. An alternative response is to put in question the strong relationship between teaching and learning, and to see the relationship as one of an evolving negotiation of content, process and outcomes, with many intervening and uncontrollable variables (see for example Berk, 1988). The appropriate strategy for the teacher may be to engage in the guided didactic conversation with the learner that Holmberg (1989: 43–6) describes rather than to refine techniques of teaching.

Activities in Distance Education

A specific area of interest that relates to interdependence is the response of learners to activities in distance-learning materials. Activities have become a standard part of distance-education material, partly following the example of the Open University. It is notable how activities have also become a very common feature of books addressed to the general readership in the field of teacher education. Lockwood (1992) speaks of learners 'degrading' activities by treating them in a cursory or tokenistic way. I think that he has identified an important issue — many (most?) users of material do not do the activities in the way expected by the designer — but I wish that he had chosen a less emotive term. 'Degradation' suggests misuse of precious objects of art by clumsy barbarians. Harris (1987: 112–14) outlines the case of Mr Wavendon, who pursued a purely instrumental policy in studying for an Open University degree. He speaks of students like this doing 'dreadful violence to even simple ideas' (p. 116). For Harris, however, the point at issue as far as instrumentalism is concerned, is 'the convergence between student strategies and the reductions and operationalisms of educational technology' (p. 118). Perhaps rather we should take the issue of instrumentalism as one of the elements in the negotiation of interdependence. An indicator of quality material might be, not so much the skilful design of the activities, as the extent to which the materials help the learners to develop the necessary autonomous attitudes and learning skills and make a conscious decision about what they want to get from an activity. Thorpe (1979: 13) reminds us:

> We should begin from the assumption that course materials are not the course; rather that the course is an annual process of interaction between students, the materials and the tutors and that, in this sense, tutors and students 'produce' courses as well as course teams.

Open Management

Finally, and perhaps at the heart of the problem, Paul (1990) argues that open learning (in the developmental sense) requires open management; in other words, that management strategies must change to serve the aims of education and specifically that *management practices in education must be driven by the values of the curriculum,* rather than the contrary being the case. Rowntree (1992: 255) spells out some of the characteristics of open management.

Two philosophies

At this point I want to reframe the idea of two traditions of open learning into a more widely applicable contrast between two approaches to teaching and learning. One could describe these two contrasting approaches as training and education (Larsen-Freeman, 1983) or control and independence (Gibbs, 1992); for the purposes of this paper I prefer to focus on the philosophical underpinning by using the terms technical-rational and critical (Zeichner, 1983; Tom, 1985). (See Table 15.4.)

Table 15.4 Approaches to teaching and learning

A technical-rational orientation	*A critical orientation*
— training — outcomes and competencies	— education — process
— planning — control	— development — independence
— standards — prescription — vocational orientation	— change — creativity — personal or political orientation
— skills and knowledge	— attitudes and values

Evans & Nation (1989: 249) argue that there is a very strong tendency for distance education to negate the values of the critical orientation:

> Distance education uses its textual, curricular and pedagogical processes to marginalise and dissolve the self-directedness of people's learning, and confines them to a system of learning which reflects and aids the reproduction of the ideological and structural conditions of society.

Harris (1987) offers an informed and incisive critique of the evolution of the Open University and comes to similar conclusions, while recognising (p. 150) that distance education and educational technology do have liberating potential. Here again distance education as a paradigm case can be seen as being at the centre of a wider educational debate.

Towards Reconciliation

The tension need not be seen so starkly. Larsen-Freeman (1983) argues that while training can stand alone, education necessarily subsumes a training component. Gibbs (1992), in an apparently different context, that of large classes in contact education, contrasts control and independence as alternative strategies. I intentionally include this reference here because it seems to me that the issue of large classes is different only in degree and not in kind from that of distance education: in both situations the student is faced with difficulty of access to teachers and learning resources and consequently experiences some alienation from the institution.

Gibbs analyses the problems that arise from the distancing of students in large classes, and identifies a set of strategies — such as objective testing, use of set books, use of learning packages — which he calls control strategies. He contrasts this approach with what he calls independence strategies, such as self assessment group work, negotiated goals, and co-operative learning. Finally he argues that control and independence strategies need not be in conflict. The ideal would be the use of control strategies by management to facilitate the aim of learner independence.

Garrison (1989: ch. 3) presents a more elaborate model, in which control is a product of the interrelationship of on the one hand, the teacher, the student and the content, and on the other hand, of the extent of the learner's achievement of autonomy, the learner's learning skills, and the support available to the learner. In Garrison's model the issue is not a choice between managerial control and the independence of the learner, but rather one of interdependence of teacher, learner and content, aimed at transferring control to the learner. He cites with approval the view of Inglis (1987) that distance education should evolve teaching methodologies that will satisfy the diversity of needs and learning styles of the students.

Garrison (1989: 40) goes on to argue for the crucial role for technology in facilitating this relationship of interdependence and the process of promoting learner autonomy. This view is shared by Holmberg (1990); Holmberg states forcefully that the role of media in distance education is a key *academic* issue, principally because high technology media facilitate the guided didactic conversation (Holmberg, 1989) that he sees as lying at the heart of good quality distance education.

Quality (2)

The argument at this point is that aims of education such as autonomy, life-long learning, the whole person, should not be seen as romantic irrelevancies in the robust managerial world of market forces. Rather, it is education which enables market forces and social processes to operate in ways that are not short-termist and self-defeating.

In this context it may be relevant to cite Barnett's recent characterisation of total quality in higher education (1992: 78–9). He argues that intrinsic to higher education are the following purposes:

- a concern with each student's autonomy, self-critical abilities, and academic competence;

- corporate responsibility for the maintenance and improvement of standards;
- a culture of critical discourse;
- a concern to make higher education available to all who can benefit from it.

Personally, I would want to add to this list a fifth purpose, which is concerned with awareness of ethical and social values of education.

Elton (1988: 223) specifies some characteristics of and necessary conditions for learner autonomy in distance education, including negotiable structures, assignments, and assessments, heavy emphasis on interaction between learner and teacher, absence of predetermined behavioural objectives. To these, we might add ideas drawn from the preceding discussion of academic counselling, the interactive role of technology, styles of management, and the deep structure of competencies, and others not touched on, such as learner networks, self-help groups, in order to constitute an account of quality that addresses itself to aims rather than to objectives, and that can be open to critical professional evaluation.

Quality in Language-Teaching Theory

Language teaching, and teacher education for language teaching, are professional areas that have a lot to offer the specification of quality in this sense; I am thinking of well-established concepts such as learner-training, learner strategies, collaborative learning, individual differences, collaborative assessment, process syllabuses, authenticity, integrative testing, self-access, group activities, critical reflection, classroom based research. These concepts constitute not only a current research agenda but also a coherent set of values. They present problems for tidy and attractive packaging in an efficient delivery system; on the other hand it would be hard to imagine colleagues in language teaching not giving considerable attention to these issues in distance material. So, as distance education has impacted in a major way on traditional higher education, so perhaps, in a less dramatic way, language teaching might contribute to the emerging reconceptualisation of distance education.

Total Quality (or Perhaps We Should Say Professional Quality)

The line of argument taken then is that for the rather complicated endeavour we are considering — language teaching (and teacher education for language teaching), in distance mode — total quality would be characterised by the state of the art in the professional field, 'delivered'[3] in such a way that managerial, technological, counselling, and teaching skills work together to serve socially enlightened aims of education. This concept might be represented by Figure 15.1.

Notes

1. BS5750 This refers to a British Standard of 'fitness of purpose' in relation to quality of course provision.
2. Total Quality Management.
3. The scare quotes around 'delivered' signal that if we are seriously concerned with Professional Quality we should be cautious about the use of language which represents alternative paradigms.

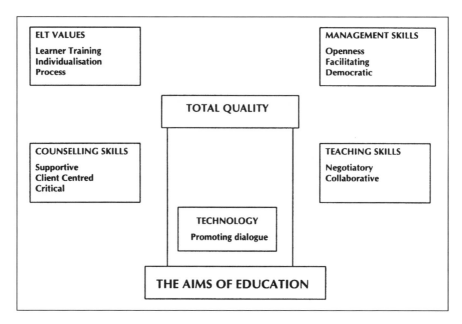

Figure 15.1 Total quality in the service of educational aims

References

Adams, M. (1991) Evaluation and educational performance: making sense of performance indicators in a managerial context. *Journal of Further and Higher Education* 15(3), 3–16.

Barnett, J. (1992) *Improving Higher Education — Total Quality Care.* Milton Keynes: Society for Research into Higher Education/Open University.

Bates, A. (ed.) (1990) *Media and Technology in European Distance Education.* Milton Keynes: EADTU/Open University.

Berk, R. (1988) Fifty reasons why student achievement gain does not mean teacher effectiveness. *Journal of Personnel Evaluation in Education* 1(4), 345–65.

Boot, R. and Hodgson, V. (1987) Open learning: meaning and experience. In Hodgson, V., Mann, S., and Snell, R. (eds) (1987): 5–15.

Boot, R. and Hodgson, V. (1988) Open learning: philosophy or expediency? *Programmed Learning and Educational Technology* 25(3), 197–204.

Burke, J. (1992) Exploring a new paradigm: research degree programme in NVQs. *Educational and Training Technology International* 29(3), 249–56.

Dickinson, L. (1992) *Learner Training for Language Learning.* Dublin: Authentik.

Elton, L. (1988) Conditions for learner autonomy at a distance. *Programmed Learning and Educational Technology* 25(3), 216–24.

Evans, T. and Nation, D. (1989) *Critical Reflections on Distance Education.* London: Falmer.

Garrison, D. (1989) *Understanding Distance Education.* London: Routledge.

Gibbs, G. (1992) Control and independence. In Gibbs, G. and Jenkins, A. (eds) (1992): 37–62.

Gibbs, G. and Jenkins, A. (eds) (1992) *Teaching Large Classes in Higher Education — How to Maintain Quality with Reduced Resources.* London: Kogan Page.

Grugeon, D. (1987) Educational counselling and open learning. In Thorpe, M. and Grugeon, D. (eds) (1987). *Open Learning for Adults.* Harlow: Longman: 195–201.

Harris, D. (1987) *Openness and Closure in Distance Education.* London: Falmer.

Hodgson, V. Mann, S., and Snell, R. (eds) (1987) *Beyond Distance Teaching — Towards Open Learning.* Milton Keynes: Society for Research into Higher Education /Open University.

Hodkinson, P. (1992) Alternative models of competence in vocational education and training. *Journal of Further and Higher Education* 16(2), 30–39.

Holmberg, B. (1989) *Theory and Practice of Distance Education.* London: Routledge.

Holmberg, B. (1990) The role of media in distance education as a key academic issue. In Bates, A. (ed.) (1990): ch. 5.

International Higher Education Standing Committee. (1988) First International Conference on Innovation and Change in Higher Education, The Place of Open and Distance Learning. Call for contributions.

Inglis, P. (1987) Distance teaching is dead! Long live distance learning. *International Council for Distance Education Bulletin* 15, 47–53.

Jevons, F. (1984) Distance education in mixed institutions: working towards parity. *Distance Education* 5(1), 24–37.

Kaye, A. and Rumble, G. (eds) (1981) *Distance Teaching for Higher and Adult Education.* London: Croom Helm/Open University.

Keegan, D. (1983) On defining distance education. In Sewart, D., Keegan, D. and Holmberg, B. (eds) (1983): 6–33.

Keegan, D. (1990) *The Foundations of Distance Education* (2nd edn). London: Croom Helm.

Larsen-Freeman, D. (1983) Training teachers or educating a teacher. In Alatis, J., Stern, H. and Strevens, P. (eds) (1983) *Applied Linguistics and the Preparation of Second Language Teachers — Towards a Rationale.* Georgetown: Georgetown University Press: 264–274.

Lockwood, F. (1992) *Activities in Self-instructional Texts.* London: Kogan Page.

Loder, C. (ed.) (1990) *Quality Assurance and Accountability in Higher Education.* London: Kogan Page/Institute of Education, University of London.

Marshall, K. (1991) NVQ's: an assessment of the 'outcomes' approach in education and training. *Journal of Further and Higher Education* 15(3), 56–64.

McGarvey, B. and Swallow, D. (1986) *Microteaching in Teacher Education and Training.* London: Croom Helm.

McNamara, D. (1992) The reform of teacher education in England and Wales: teacher competence; panacea or rhetoric? *Journal of Education for Teaching* 18(3), 273–85.

Muller, D. and Funnell, P. (1992) An exploration of the concept of quality in vocational education and training. *Educational Training and Training Technology International* 29(3), 257–61.

Oxford, R. (1990) *Language Learning Strategies.* New York: Newbury House.

Paul, R. (1990) *Open Learning and Open Management: Leadership and Integrity in Distance Education.* London: Kogan Page.

Rowntree, D. (1992) *Exploring Open and Distance Learning.* London: Kogan Page

Sewart, D., Keegan, D. and Holmberg, B. (eds) (1983) *Distance Education: International Perspectives.* London: Croom Helm.

Snell, R. (1987) The challenge of painful and unpleasant emotions. In Hodgson, V., Mann, S. and Snell, R. (eds) (1987): 59–72.

Thorpe, M. (1988) *Evaluating Open and Distance Learning.* Harlow: Longman.

Tom, A. (1985) Inquiring into inquiry-oriented teacher education. *Journal of Teacher Education* 36(5), 35–44.

Yorke, M. (1992) Quality in higher education. *Journal of Further and Higher Education* 16(2), 90–104.

Zeichner, K. (1983) Alternative paradigms of teacher education. *Journal of Teacher Education* 34(3), 3–9.

Index

DL=distance learning/education
FtF=face-to-face /direct contact teaching
CMC=computer-mediated communication